THE Creative LUNCH BOX

THE Creative LUNCH BOX

Easy, Nutritious, and Inviting Meals for Your Child

Ellen Klavan

Illustrations by Meg Hartigan

Crown Publishers, Inc. New York

The tables entitled Basic Four Food Guide for Children and Basic Four Food Guide for Adolescents were reprinted with permission of Boston Children's Hospital, with Susan Baker and Roberta Henry, *Parents' Guide to Nutrition*, © 1987 by Boston Children's Hospital. Reprinted with permission of Addison-Wesley Publishing Co., Inc., Reading, Massachusetts.

Published by Crown Publishers, Inc., 201 East 50th Street,
New York, New York, 10022. Member of the Crown Publishing Group.
CROWN is a trademark of Crown Publishers, Inc.

Manufactured in the United States of America

Library of Congress Cataloging-in-Publication Data

Klavan, Ellen.
The creative lunch box : easy, nutritious, and inviting meals for your child / by Ellen Klavan. — 1st ed.
p. cm.
Includes index.
1. Lunch box cookery. I. Title.
TX735.K58 1991 90-22707
641.5'3—dc20 CIP

ISBN 0-517-57730-5

Book design by Nancy Kenmore

10 9 8 7 6 5 4 3 2 1
First Edition

For Drew

the way kids eat the lunches we pack for them. Here are a few lunch box realities.

If you want your child to eat his lunch, you've got to send him to school with food that he likes. Kids want to have control over what they eat. And well they should: It's your child's body, his taste buds, and his hunger that is being met by the food he eats. The more children are allowed to select foods they enjoy for themselves, the less likely they are to develop food fads or engage their parents in struggles over food. This is true at home and it's especially true away from home, where children have the most control over what they eat. There's no point in sending your child to school with a plum in his lunch box if you know he doesn't like plums. Send him to school with a fruit he will eat, even if it's the same fruit every day for a month.

Your child will only eat as much food as he feels like eating when he sits down for lunch. You can fill his lunch box with his favorite foods, but he'll eat only as much as he is hungry for. Don't be alarmed if you find he's only eating half a sandwich and skipping his apple. Children are good at regulating their own food intake. If he's very hungry after school, he might eat the apple on the way home. Or he may ask for a snack when he gets home. Either way, as long as you provide him with foods he likes, he won't go undernourished.

Your child will probably only eat food that he feels comfortable eating in the cafeteria setting. While there are certainly some children who are brave enough to make an independent stand, most kids are greatly influenced by peer pres-

Contents

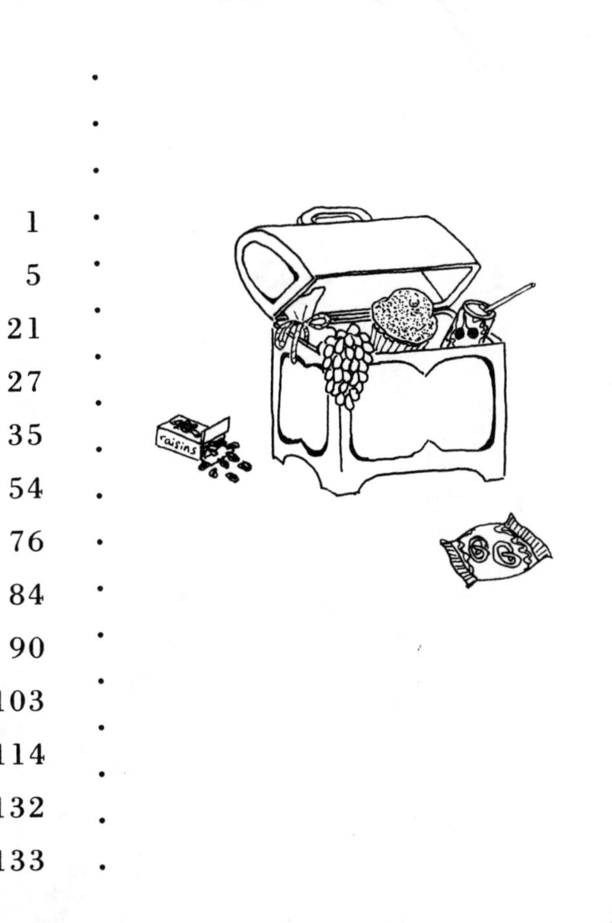

1
Lunch Box Realities

When your child brings his lunch to school, he carries a little piece of home with him. Naturally, you want him to open his lunch box and find a nourishing, tasty meal that reminds him that he is loved and cherished. Perhaps you've chosen to send his lunch to school instead of having him buy a cafeteria lunch because you want to ensure that he gets a balanced, healthy meal. But how sure are you that he's eating the meal you've packed for him?

Let's face it. You can control what goes into your child's lunch box every day, but you *can't* control what goes into your child. Once he's actually sitting at the cafeteria table with his friends, his open lunch box before him, anything can happen.

You'll know what I mean if you've ever opened your child's lunch box at the end of the day and found a bizarre collection of ancient artifacts inside. One Wednesday afternoon, for example, one mother found in her son's lunch box the following items: a slice of ham and a slice of cheese balled up together in a plastic bag (he'd eaten just the bread from his sandwich), two pieces of celery licked clean of peanut butter, three or four cookie crumbs (he'd had a hearty appetite for dessert), and an almost-full thermos of milk.

Another mother was sure she'd hit on the right combination of foods for her daughter when the girl's lunch box began coming home empty every day. It was only after a few weeks that she discovered that her daughter was trading Mom's lovingly prepared cucumber and sprouts on whole-wheat bread sandwiches across the table for Hostess Twinkies and other sugary treats!

Keeping these examples in mind, we can draw a few conclusions about sure, especially during the elementary school years. Although your child may love eating cold broccoli spears at home, he may not be comfortable eating this food at school. He may become anxious about eating anything that appears "babyish" (applesauce might fit into this category, for instance) or "nerdy" (almost anything could fit into this category, depending on the whims of your child's particular school culture). Vegetable soup with dumplings brought to school in a wide-mouthed thermos may be accepted at one school and ridiculed at another. It's important to respect your child's views on these matters and help him find foods that he believes are acceptable fare among his social set.

Given these realities, the task you face is to find foods that meet your nutritional standards *and* suit your child's taste and social standards as well. With a little help from the recipes in this book, you shouldn't have much trouble accomplishing that goal. Keep these points in mind for lunch box planning:

Consult your child about what goes into his lunch box. As much as possible, involve your child in the preparation of his own lunch. The recipes in this book are designed to be easy enough for school-age children to make themselves. Set aside a time—whether it's the night before or (if you're early risers!) in the morning—to prepare lunch together.

Try out any new meals at home before you pack them in your child's lunch box. Kids generally like surprises, but most won't appreciate finding something new and unfamiliar in their lunch boxes at noon.

Take your child's eating habits into account. You know your child pretty well. Is he likely to race through his lunch so he can get out to the recess yard as fast as possible? If so, you want to give him a lunch that he can consume easily and quickly. The Super-Hero Sandwich (page 45) would be a good choice for him. Or does your child enjoy sitting and chatting with friends over lunch? Would he appreciate a more sophisticated meal? If so, the Do-It-Yourself Salad (page 72) may appeal to him.

Think about what else your child will be eating during the day. If you've served cantaloupe for breakfast and are planning a fruit salad for tonight's dessert, you don't have to worry about providing a fruit for today's lunch. If he didn't drink any milk this morning, you may want to add some cheese to today's lunch. Chapter 2, "Commonsense Nutrition," will help you figure out which foods your child needs every day.

2

Commonsense Nutrition

It's a challenge, all right. When your child is bombarded with television advertisements for candy, potato chips, and fruit roll-ups, when her friends are bringing sugary fruit pies to school, when your child's own taste buds cry out for junk . . . it's a challenge to get healthy foods into your child.

It's a challenge, too, to figure out just what a healthy diet is. If you're like me, you probably have a hard time calling to mind just what the difference is between a vitamin and a mineral. Quick: Which vitamins are in a banana? And which vitamin is supposed to be good for your eyesight? Which one is good for your skin? You could make yourself crazy trying to include every mineral and vitamin under the sun in your child's daily diet.

Fortunately, if you rely on your old friends the basic four food groups (remember health class in junior high?) and your own common sense, you'll be able to put together menus that are both nutritious and tasty.

The Basic Four

Here, in case your memory of the seventh grade is a little sketchy, is a list of the basic four food groups. The tables on pages 8 to 11 show you how much of each food group your child needs each day.

1. *Meat or Equivalent Protein:* Meat is obvious: poultry, fish, beef, pork, and lamb. Most Americans eat far more meat than they need. Consult the tables to find the right amount of meat for your child.

Contents

1
Lunch Box Realities

When your child brings his lunch to school, he carries a little piece of home with him. Naturally, you want him to open his lunch box and find a nourishing, tasty meal that reminds him that he is loved and cherished. Perhaps you've chosen to send his lunch to school instead of having him buy a cafeteria lunch because you want to ensure that he gets a balanced, healthy meal. But how sure are you that he's eating the meal you've packed for him?

Let's face it. You can control what goes into your child's lunch box every day, but you *can't* control what goes into your child. Once he's actually sitting at the cafeteria table with his friends, his open lunch box before him, anything can happen.

You'll know what I mean if you've ever opened your child's lunch box at the end of the day and found a bizarre collection of ancient artifacts inside. One Wednesday afternoon, for example, one mother found in her son's lunch box the following items: a slice of ham and a slice of cheese balled up together in a plastic bag (he'd eaten just the bread from his sandwich), two pieces of celery licked clean of peanut butter, three or four cookie crumbs (he'd had a hearty appetite for dessert), and an almost-full thermos of milk.

Another mother was sure she'd hit on the right combination of foods for her daughter when the girl's lunch box began coming home empty every day. It was only after a few weeks that she discovered that her daughter was trading Mom's lovingly prepared cucumber and sprouts on whole-wheat bread sandwiches across the table for Hostess Twinkies and other sugary treats!

Keeping these examples in mind, we can draw a few conclusions about the way kids eat the lunches we pack for them. Here are a few lunch box realities.

If you want your child to eat his lunch, you've got to send him to school with food that he likes. Kids want to have control over what they eat. And well they should: It's your child's body, his taste buds, and his hunger that is being met by the food he eats. The more children are allowed to select foods they enjoy for themselves, the less likely they are to develop food fads or engage their parents in struggles over food. This is true at home and it's especially true away from home, where children have the most control over what they eat. There's no point in sending your child to school with a plum in his lunch box if you know he doesn't like plums. Send him to school with a fruit he will eat, even if it's the same fruit every day for a month.

Your child will only eat as much food as he feels like eating when he sits down for lunch. You can fill his lunch box with his favorite foods, but he'll eat only as much as he is hungry for. Don't be alarmed if you find he's only eating half a sandwich and skipping his apple. Children are good at regulating their own food intake. If he's very hungry after school, he might eat the apple on the way home. Or he may ask for a snack when he gets home. Either way, as long as you provide him with foods he likes, he won't go undernourished.

Your child will probably only eat food that he feels comfortable eating in the cafeteria setting. While there are certainly some children who are brave enough to make an independent stand, most kids are greatly influenced by peer pressure, especially during the elementary school years. Although your child may love eating cold broccoli spears at home, he may not be comfortable eating this food at school. He may become anxious about eating anything that appears "babyish" (applesauce might fit into this category, for instance) or "nerdy" (almost anything could fit into this category, depending on the whims of your child's particular school culture). Vegetable soup with dumplings brought to school in a wide-mouthed thermos may be accepted at one school and ridiculed at another. It's important to respect your child's views on these matters and help him find foods that he believes are acceptable fare among his social set.

Given these realities, the task you face is to find foods that meet your nutritional standards *and* suit your child's taste and social standards as well. With a little help from the recipes in this book, you shouldn't have much trouble accomplishing that goal. Keep these points in mind for lunch box planning:

Consult your child about what goes into his lunch box. As much as possible, involve your child in the preparation of his own lunch. The recipes in this book are designed to be easy enough for school-age children to make themselves. Set aside a time—whether it's the night before or (if you're early risers!) in the morning—to prepare lunch together.

Try out any new meals at home before you pack them in your child's lunch box. Kids generally like surprises, but most won't appreciate finding something new and unfamiliar in their lunch boxes at noon.

Take your child's eating habits into account. You know your child pretty well. Is he likely to race through his lunch so he can get out to the recess yard as fast as possible? If so, you want to give him a lunch that he can consume easily and quickly. The Super-Hero Sandwich (page 45) would be a good choice for him. Or does your child enjoy sitting and chatting with friends over lunch? Would he appreciate a more sophisticated meal? If so, the Do-It-Yourself Salad (page 72) may appeal to him.

Think about what else your child will be eating during the day. If you've served cantaloupe for breakfast and are planning a fruit salad for tonight's dessert, you don't have to worry about providing a fruit for today's lunch. If he didn't drink any milk this morning, you may want to add some cheese to today's lunch. Chapter 2, "Commonsense Nutrition," will help you figure out which foods your child needs every day.

2

Commonsense Nutrition

It's a challenge, all right. When your child is bombarded with television advertisements for candy, potato chips, and fruit roll-ups, when her friends are bringing sugary fruit pies to school, when your child's own taste buds cry out for junk . . . it's a challenge to get healthy foods into your child.

It's a challenge, too, to figure out just what a healthy diet is. If you're like me, you probably have a hard time calling to mind just what the difference is between a vitamin and a mineral. Quick: Which vitamins are in a banana? And which vitamin is supposed to be good for your eyesight? Which one is good for your skin? You could make yourself crazy trying to include every mineral and vitamin under the sun in your child's daily diet.

Fortunately, if you rely on your old friends the basic four food groups (remember health class in junior high?) and your own common sense, you'll be able to put together menus that are both nutritious and tasty.

The Basic Four

Here, in case your memory of the seventh grade is a little sketchy, is a list of the basic four food groups. The tables on pages 8 to 11 show you how much of each food group your child needs each day.

1. *Meat or Equivalent Protein:* Meat is obvious: poultry, fish, beef, pork, and lamb. Most Americans eat far more meat than they need. Consult the tables to find the right amount of meat for your child.

Like meat, eggs and dairy products (milk, cheese, and yogurt) contain "complete," or "high-quality," protein. "Incomplete," or "low-quality," protein is abundant in these nonanimal foods: seeds, nuts (including the ever-popular peanut butter), and protein-rich legumes, such as beans or peas. See A Vegetarian Diet, at right, for more information on feeding your child nonanimal protein.

2. *Grains:* This group includes any food made from wheat, oats, rye, rice, or other grains. You probably won't have much trouble getting your child to eat something from a list that includes cereal, bread, crackers, muffins, pasta, tortillas, and rice.

3. *Dairy Products:* Long after her babyhood is over, your child still needs plenty of milk. If she doesn't like milk, she can eat equivalent amounts of cheese, yogurt, and, on special occasions, ice cream.

4. *Fruits and Vegetables:* This group includes all the fruits and all the vegetables except those (such as beans or peas) that double as protein. For many kids, this is the most "yucky" food group. Remember that equivalent servings of juice, which is often more acceptable to kids, can replace servings of fruits and vegetables.

Ideally, your child should have some foods from each of the basic four groups every day. The following chart indicates the proportions that, in the best of all possible worlds, your child should consume each day.

A Vegetarian Diet

Your child can thrive on a vegetarian diet that includes dairy products, providing you take pains to ensure that she receives all the protein, vitamins, and minerals that she will not be getting from meat and eggs. The four main sources of nonanimal protein are legumes, seeds and nuts, vegetables, and grains. Blended in the right combinations, these low-quality proteins can yield a high-quality protein that is the equivalent of meat. For example, a peanut butter sandwich offers such a combination, as does meatless chili with rice. If your family maintains a strictly vegetarian diet, consult with your child's pediatrician about ways of ensuring that your child receives adequate nutrition.

Basic Four Food Guide for Children

• • •

Preschoolers and School-Aged Children:
4–10 years
(1,700–2,100 calories a day)

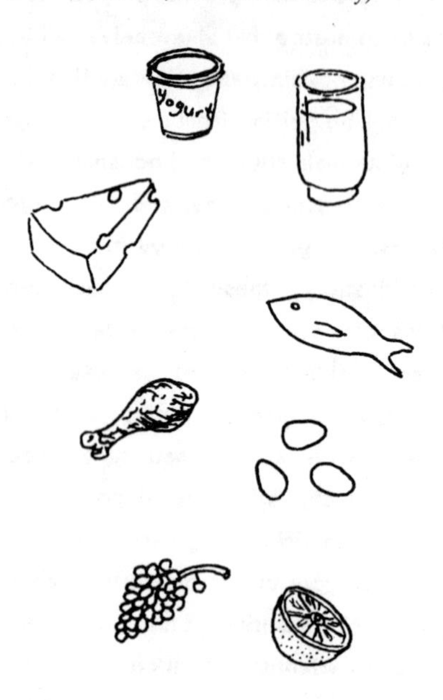

Food Group	*Recommended Number of Servings*	*Average Serving Size*
Milk (or equivalent)	4	
Milk, preferably low fat or skim		3/4–1 cup
Powdered milk		3–4 tbsp.
Cheese		3/4–1 1/2 oz.
Cottage cheese		3/4–1 cup
Yogurt		3/4–1 cup
Meat, fish, poultry (or equivalent)	2 or more	2–3 oz.
Eggs		1 whole
Peanut butter		2–3 tbsp.
Cooked dried peas or beans		1/2–3/4 cup
Luncheon meat		2 slices
Vegetables and fruits	4 or more	
Citrus fruits (vitamin C source)	1 or more	
Orange or grapefruit juice		1/2–1 cup
Strawberries		1 cup
Tomatoes or tomato juice		1/2–1 cup

Food Group	*Recommended Number of Servings*	*Average Serving Size*
Vegetables and fruits (*continued*)		
Yellow or green vegetable or fruit (vitamin A source)	1 or more	
Broccoli		1/4 cup
Spinach		1/4 cup
Carrots		1/4 cup
Squash		1/4 cup
Cantaloupe		1/4–1/2 fruit
Apricots		5–8 halves
Other fruits and vegetables	2 or more	
Fresh, frozen, canned fruits and vegetables		1/2 cup
Potato, turnip, most whole vegetables		1/2–1 veg.
Apple, banana, most whole fruits		1/2–1 fruit

Food Group	*Recommended Number of Servings*	*Average Serving Size*
Breads and cereals (whole grain or enriched)	4 or more	
Bread		1–2 slices
Dry cereal (unsweetened)		1 cup
Cooked cereal, rice, pasta		½ cup
Others (to meet calorie needs)	as needed	
Butter, margarine, mayonnaise, oil		1–2 tbsp.
Desserts		
Pudding		½ cup
Ice cream or ice milk		1 cup
Cookies		2–3 medium
Cake		1 oz.
Pie		1½ oz.
Sugar, honey, molasses, jelly, jam		2 tbsp.

Basic Four Food Guide for Adolescents

Ages 11–17 Years
(2,100–2,800 calories a day)

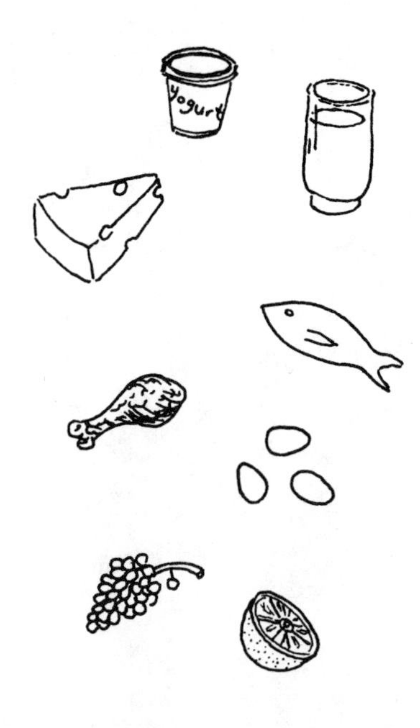

Food Group	*Recommended Number of Servings*	*Average Serving Size*
Milk (or equivalent)	4 or more	
Milk, preferably low fat or skim		1 cup
Powdered milk		4 tbsp.
Cheese		1½ oz.
Cottage cheese		1 cup
Yogurt		1 cup
Meat, fish, poultry (or equivalent)	3 or more	3–5 oz.
Eggs		1–2 whole
Peanut butter		3 tbsp.
Cooked dried peas or beans		1–1½ cups
Luncheon meat		2–3 slices
Vegetables and fruit	4 or more	½–1 cup
Citrus fruits (vitamin C source)	1 or more	
Orange or grapefruit juice		1 cup
Strawberries		1½ cups
Tomatoes or tomato juice		1 cup

Food Group	*Recommended Number of Servings*	*Average Serving Size*
Vegetables and fruits (*continued*)		
Yellow or green vegetable or fruit (vitamin A source)	1 or more	
Broccoli		½ cup
Spinach		½ cup
Carrots		½ cup
Squash		½ cup
Cantaloupe		½ fruit
Apricots		8–10 halves
Other fruits and vegetables	2 or more	
Fresh, frozen, canned fruits and vegetables		½ cup
Potato, turnip, most whole vegetables		1 veg.
Apple, banana, most whole fruits		1 fruit

Food Group	*Recommended Number of Servings*	*Average Serving Size*
Breads and cereals (whole grain or enriched)	4 or more	
Bread		2 slices
Dry cereal (unsweetened)		1–1½ cups
Cooked cereal, rice, pasta		1 cup or more
Others (to meet calorie needs)	as needed	
Butter, margarine, mayonnaise, oil		2–4 tbsp.
Desserts		
Pudding		½–1 cup
Ice cream or ice milk		1–1½ cups
Cookies		3–4 medium
Cake		1½ oz.
Pie		2 oz.
Sugar, honey, molasses, jelly, jam		2–4 tbsp.

Did You Take Your Vitamin?

To make sure your child receives the vitamins and minerals she needs every day, see that she takes a multivitamin. You might consider keeping your child's vitamins on the breakfast table, to remind her to take one each morning.

The Self-Selection Theory

Most contemporary nutritionists believe that when children are offered an array of healthful foods, they will self-select a diet that meets their nutritional needs. This means that if you simply offer your child foods from the basic four groups every day, she will eat the ones that she needs. There's no need for you to stand over her counting up every gram of protein and adding up the day's mineral intake.

Kids don't necessarily have to drink exactly four cups of milk (or eat four or more vegetables, two or more servings of meat or other protein, and so on) every day to eat healthily. The self-selecting theory holds that *over time* most children select a balanced diet that, were it broken down day by day, would approximate the breakdowns given in the preceding charts.

This whole system will fall apart, however, if you consistently offer your child foods that aren't nutritious. Given a choice between steamed asparagus or potato chips, or between a carrot muffin and a candy bar, your child will usually self-select an unhealthy diet. A certain amount of junk food is a fact of life in most American families (it certainly is in mine!), but keeping a lid on junk is important if you want your child to have a balanced diet.

The Nutritious Lunch

The easiest way to ensure that your child gets a healthy array of choices from the basic four food groups each day is to offer food from each group at every meal. Your child doesn't necessarily have to eat a wide variety of foods, although that would be ideal. If she's hooked on oranges, there's no need to try to persuade her to bring a grapefruit to school. If the only vegetable she'll eat is celery, keep the celery coming. Remember to offer alternatives from time to time, though, in case your child has a change of heart.

The Bad Guys: Salt, Sugar, and More

Most of the foods that we think of as bad for children are really only bad for them if they are eaten in excess. A certain amount of fat, for example, is essential to everyone's diet. So is a certain amount of salt. A child can live without refined sugar, but she doesn't really have to. Too much of any of those foods, though, can distort a child's diet, making it hard for her to self-select the healthful foods she needs and creating the potential for other health problems as well.

Fresh, Canned, or Frozen?

The very best way to serve fruits and vegetables is fresh from the vine, raw or lightly steamed. By the time fruits and vegetables arrive at the market, travel to your home, and sit in your refrigerator for a week, they are far from perfectly fresh. In some cases, frozen or canned fruits and vegetables that have been processed soon after picking may contain more nutrients than wilted or stale fresh foods. Some nutrients are lost during freezing and more are lost during canning, but both frozen and canned fruits and vegetables are nutritious and healthful for your child. Do, however, avoid buying fruits packed in heavy syrup.

The nutritional bad guys crop up most frequently in junk food—in fatty potato chips and sugary granola bars and foods like those "cheese" crackers that are laced with a dazzling array of food additives. If you buy fresh foods and carefully check the labels of the prepared foods you buy, you can easily avoid excessive amounts of these ingredients.

Here's what you need to know about the nutritional bad guys:

Salt. Every child needs a certain amount of sodium in her diet, although experts don't agree on the exact amount that is needed. It's almost impossible to get too little salt, however, given the amount of sodium that is regularly used in cooking, as a condiment, and as an additive in prepared foods. It is possible, however, to get far more sodium than is healthful. If your child consumes too much sodium, she may be vulnerable to health problems, such as heart and kidney disease, when she is an adult. Check the labels of the foods you buy and avoid those that have a high sodium content; look for the word *salt* and for any variation on the word *sodium*—sodium nitrate, for instance. Don't season your child's food with salt.

Sugar. Unlike salt, refined sugar has no redeeming nutritional value. It provides empty calories and contributes to tooth decay and obesity. Some experts and parents have noted a link between sugar consumption and aggressive or excessively active behavior, though this has yet to be proven definitively. Don't be fooled by claims that honey, maple syrup, molasses, or brown sugar is better for your child than white sugar—these foods are nutritional equivalents of white sugar. Sugar is used as a food additive in a wide range of foods including ketchup, breakfast cereal, and some brands of peanut butter. How much sugar you decide to allow your child is a personal decision.

Artificial Sweeteners. Sorry, but I can't recommend that you use artificial sweeteners instead of sugar. I know it's tempting to use the latest artificial sweetening product, aspartame (marketed as NutraSweet®), because it tastes almost as good as sugar. But consumer advocates claim that this product has not been adequately tested. Based on animal research, some scientists argue that aspartame can cause brain damage in children.

Fats. Like salt, fat is an essential part of everyone's diet. More than adults, children need fat because it gives them energy and helps them grow. If your child eats the amounts of meat and dairy products plus extra fats listed in the charts, she'll get all the fat she needs. Unfortunately, she'll probably consume more fat than she needs when she eats french fries, chocolate, and other fatty foods. Try to ensure that any additional fats consumed are polyunsaturated and come from sources such as safflower, sunflower, corn, and soybean oil. Less healthful are saturated fats, which come from meat and dairy products, or from hydrogenated fats, such as coconut oil and palm oil. (If your child is overweight, consult her doctor. A reduced-fat diet may be recommended.)

Cholesterol. The C-word! You'd have to have spent the last decade in a rabbit hole not to know that cholesterol has become public health enemy number one.

Cholesterol is a fatlike substance found in meat, poultry, dairy products, and eggs. It is only bad when consumed in excess. Children need a certain amount of cholesterol in their diets. Again, if you follow the preceding dietary guidelines, you probably won't overdose your child with cholesterol. Some experts recommend limiting children to three egg yolks a week, since egg yolk contains a whopping 275 milligrams of cholesterol. By the time your child is an adolescent, you should begin to restrict her cholesterol intake to 300 milligrams daily. Unlike butter, margarine contains no cholesterol—it can be substituted for butter in almost any recipe. (*Note:* If your family has a history of heart disease, tell your child's doctor. A reduced-cholesterol diet may be recommended.)

Food Additives. Like cholesterol, the term *food additive* has, in recent years, earned a bad name that is only partly deserved. An additive is anything that has been added to a food during processing and packaging. Here are some of the kinds of additives you will commonly find listed on food product labels:

> *Flavoring*. Added to make food taste better, the most common flavorings are salt and sugar. Two flavor enhancers to especially avoid are MSG (monosodium glutamate) and caffeine.
>
> *Nutrients*. These are added to a product either because natural nutrients have been lost during processing or simply to make the product more desirable to the buyer. In general, nutrients indeed enhance the nutritional value of food.

Preservatives. Preservatives prevent food spoilage and give food products a longer shelf life. Without them, we would risk food poisoning and would have to rely more heavily on fresh foods. Most preservatives are commonly acknowledged to be useful. Consumer groups have tried unsuccessfully to ban the use of nitrates and nitrites (commonly used in pork products and smoked foods, including lunch meats), which may be dangerous when consumed in excess. Limit your use of foods that have been processed with nitrates or nitrites.

Color. Color makes apples redder and oranges more orangey. While many natural colors are considered safe, consumer advocates point to potential health hazards resulting from consumption of virtually all of the synthetically manufactured food dyes. The Food and Drug Administration (FDA) has banned the use of some of these dyes, but many remain in common usage.

Emulsifiers, stabilizers, and thickening agents. These additives change the texture of food.

In theory, the FDA evaluates additives that are used in commercially processed foods and restricts the use of any that are unhealthy for human consumption. In practice, dangerous additives do sometimes get through the cracks. The best way to protect your child is to emphasize fresh and homemade foods in your daily meal planning.

Watch out for deceptive labeling that makes processed food look like something it's not. Here are some of the terms that may fool you:

Natural. This word gives the impression that the food you are buying is healthful and nutritious. But an "all-natural" product may contain excessive amounts of sugar, fat, and salt.

Organic. On the positive side, organic foods haven't been sprayed with pesticides and they have been grown in soil that hasn't been treated with chemical fertilizers. On the negative side, organic foods tend to be more expensive and they may lack nutrients contained in foods that have been chemically fertilized.

Health food. The term *health* is used very loosely. Check the label to make sure the product meets *your* standards of good health.

Cholesterol-free. Just because a product doesn't contain cholesterol doesn't mean it's low in fats.

Sugar-free. A product that is sugar-free may nevertheless contain a sugar derivative like sorbitol or xylitol, or it may contain an artificial sweetener.

Lite. Just because a product has this misspelled version of the word *light* on its label doesn't mean it is especially nutritious. The term may be intended to convey the idea that the product has fewer calories, less sugar, less salt, or less fat than its non-"lite" counterpart. Check the ingredients and nutritional information to find out exactly what's "lite" about this product.

3

Packing It All In

Almost as important as *what* you pack in your child's lunch box is *how* you pack it. Careful packing ensures that your child's food is free of harmful bacteria and is safe to eat. Careful packing also ensures that the food arrives in good condition, not squished up in a ball in the corner of your child's lunch box.

Avoid Spoilage

Think of all the foods that you commonly keep in your refrigerator. Those are the foods that can spoil between the time your child leaves your house and when he sits down to eat in the cafeteria. Any time perishable food is left out in temperatures over 60 degrees, harmful bacteria can grow. On a winter's day, if your child walked to school with his lunch, left it by an open window all morning, and then ate it as soon as he got to the cafeteria, it probably wouldn't spoil. But even when the weather is cold, most children travel in heated school buses and spend the morning (with their lunches) in heated classrooms. So take steps to avoid spoilage regardless of the weather.

Avoiding spoilage begins even before you pack your child's lunch. Take these precautions when you're preparing his lunch:

Keep your hands and work surface clean. This goes for your child's hands too, if he's helping to make his lunch. Bacteria from dirty hands, work surfaces, or utensils can multiply in your child's lunch box.

Recycled Containers

You don't have to buy plastic containers for your child's lunch. Just save the containers from the products listed below. After you wash them thoroughly, you can use them to pack your child's lunch. He can either bring them home to be used again or throw them out after lunch.

- Cottage cheese
- Yogurt
- Sour cream
- Cream cheese
- Peanut butter
- Dip
- Ricotta cheese
- Soft margarine

Note: Don't send glass containers—they could break. Never use containers from medicine, other pharmaceutical products, or cleaning products.

Pack the lunch box strategically. When your child's lunch box is open on the counter, pack it from the bottom up. Put in his thermos and any plastic containers first and then layer the remaining food upward, with the heaviest foods on the bottom. Use a couple of napkins to fill in any blank spaces. The less empty space you have in the box, the better.

Keep your child's lunch box and thermos clean. It's not enough to just dump out the crumbs. You need to scrub out the lunch box and thermos (and any other packing containers) with hot soapy water.

Use only clean plastic bags and other wrappings. If you're naturally frugal, you may tend to save the plastic bags your vegetables come in and to reuse aluminum foil and other wrappings. But food residues on these wrappings may cause bacteria to grow in your child's lunch box, so avoid this practice.

To ensure that your child's lunch doesn't spoil, find a way of keeping it cool. Here are some ways to do that:

Use an ice pack. Buy a couple of commercial ice packs, so you'll always have one in the freezer. Place a frozen pack in your child's lunch box. Some lunch boxes (notably the Ice Man lunch box) have a built-in compartment for the ice pack.

Freeze a juice. Put a box of juice in the freezer and then pack it frozen with your child's lunch. By the time he sits down to eat, the juice will have thawed so he can drink it with his nice, fresh lunch.

Freeze a yogurt. This favorite food freezes well too.

Pack frozen foods. Breads and muffins, for example, freeze well, as do chicken drumsticks. Put a frozen muffin in your child's lunch and it should have thawed by lunchtime. Using frozen bread will help keep your child's sandwich fresh.

On-the-Way-Home Noshing

If your child is like many, he probably gets hungry after school. If he can't wait to get home and have a snack, he may dip into his lunch box for a bite to eat. Unfortunately, even the best-protected lunch may no longer be safe to eat at three o'clock. Try to educate your child about which foods are safe to eat at the end of the day. (A peanut butter sandwich should be fine, for example, while an egg salad sandwich could be risky.) You might also pack something especially for after school, like some crackers or a bag of GORP (see page 112), or an orange.

But frozen bread or a frozen muffin isn't enough to keep an entire lunch box cold.

Use a good thermos. Test your child's thermos to make sure it keeps his drinks cold (or hot). Some thermoses that come with children's lunch boxes aren't as effective as they should be. Use a wide-mouthed thermos to pack salads and other foods that you want to keep cold.

Precool your child's thermos. Keep his thermos in the freezer overnight or rinse it with ice-cold water before filling it.

You can also keep food fresh by keeping it hot. For hot drinks or hot meals (like the Chili and Rice on page 78), use a conventional or wide-mouthed thermos. (Preheat the thermos by rinsing it with boiling water.) Make sure the food or drink you pour into the thermos is piping hot.

When you're packing both hot and cold foods in your child's lunch box, insulate them from one another. For example, if you're sending Hot Spiced Apple Juice (page 87), crackers, and a salad, pack the crackers between the hot thermos and the cold one. Or use a thick piece of cardboard as a divider.

Another way of ensuring that foods don't spoil is by using prepackaged foods, such as individually packaged applesauce or individual cans of fruit salad (see page 108).

Note: Certain foods are especially vulnerable to bacteria. Be very careful when packing foods containing meat, poultry, eggs, milk, and cream cheese.

Squish Prevention Strategies

I can well remember the feeling of opening my lunch box to find a squishy mess inside. My sandwich would be smushed flat and then curled back on itself, the peanut butter from my peanut butter and celery would be smeared all over its plastic wrap, and my plum would be a pulpy mess!

Making sure your child's lunch doesn't get mashed into a pulp will help to ensure that he eats it. Here's what you can do to prevent squish:

Use plastic containers. Manufacturers have created containers in practically every shape and size. There's a sandwich-size container as well as containers that are just right for salads, bite-size snacks, fruits, and other goodies. The challenge here is to persuade your child to remember to bring the containers home and not throw them away with the uneaten part of his lunch.

Use firm ingredients. A peach is more likely to squish than an orange. By the same token, a sandwich made of Wonder Bread is a lot more likely to squish than one made of a pita pocket or a hero roll. Use the anti-sog strategies suggested on page 50.

Wrap fruits and vegetables carefully. If you send a plum or other squishy food in your child's lunch, wrap it in several layers of paper towels and then put it in a plastic bag. Wrap cut vegetables in damp paper towels to keep them from drying out.

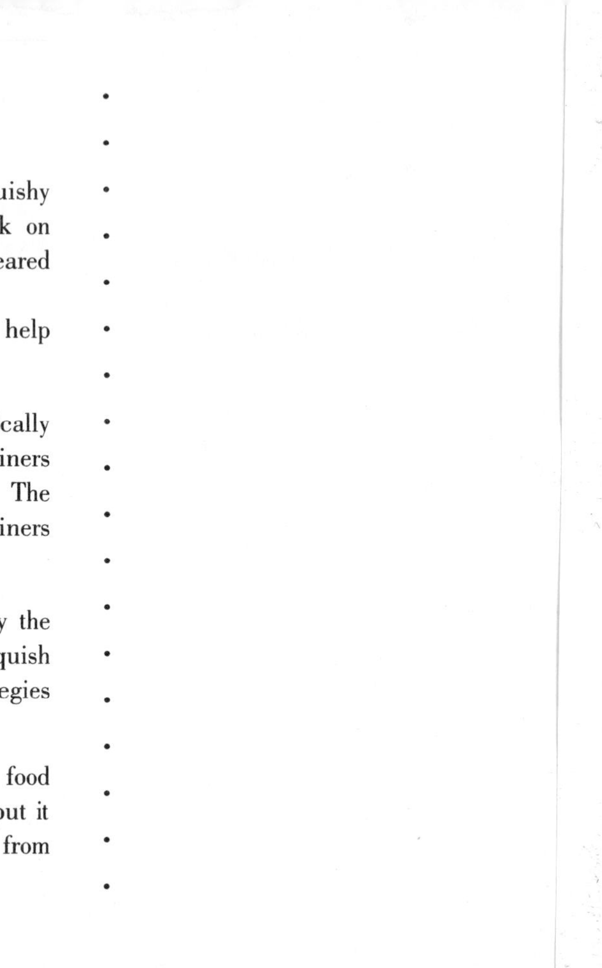

4

Add Some Fun

Riddles to Go

Send your child a riddle in her lunch and she'll have something to laugh about and share with her friends. In case you're feeling uninspired one morning, here are some grade-school winners.

Q. What's round and red and goes up and down?

A. A tomato in an elevator.

Q. What's black and white and green and black and white?

A. Two zebras fighting over a pickle.

Q. What kind of room has no walls, no floor, and no ceiling?

A. A mushroom.

You can make your child's lunch really special by packing in a few extras. You certainly don't have to do this kind of thing every day, but once in a while, finding something extra in her lunch box is a nice treat for your child.

Here are some of the ways you can make your child's lunch more inviting:

Tie it with a bow. After you've wrapped your child's sandwich in plastic, gift-wrap it! Or wrap it in the colored plastic wraps that are now available. This is a nice idea for birthdays or other special occasions.

Stickers. Use colorful stickers to seal the plastic wrap on your child's sandwich and other foods. You might also want to pack a few stickers in your child's lunch as a present.

Save those condiments. Next time you're at a fast food restaurant, save your unopened packages of ketchup, mustard, pepper, and so on. As needed, you can pack them in your child's lunch.

Use colorful paper products. A colored paper napkin will brighten up your child's day. Around the holidays, pack seasonal napkins. You might also try a colorful paper plate or a paper doily to use as a placemat. A heart-shaped one would be perfect for Valentine's Day!

Send a little present. You could send your child a small gift, such as a new pencil or eraser or small figure of one of her favorite characters. Buy some packs of party favors and send them one at a time, as the spirit moves you.

Keep your child's lunch box and thermos clean. It's not enough to just dump out the crumbs. You need to scrub out the lunch box and thermos (and any other packing containers) with hot soapy water.

Use only clean plastic bags and other wrappings. If you're naturally frugal, you may tend to save the plastic bags your vegetables come in and to reuse aluminum foil and other wrappings. But food residues on these wrappings may cause bacteria to grow in your child's lunch box, so avoid this practice.

To ensure that your child's lunch doesn't spoil, find a way of keeping it cool. Here are some ways to do that:

Use an ice pack. Buy a couple of commercial ice packs, so you'll always have one in the freezer. Place a frozen pack in your child's lunch box. Some lunch boxes (notably the Ice Man lunch box) have a built-in compartment for the ice pack.

Freeze a juice. Put a box of juice in the freezer and then pack it frozen with your child's lunch. By the time he sits down to eat, the juice will have thawed so he can drink it with his nice, fresh lunch.

Freeze a yogurt. This favorite food freezes well too.

Pack frozen foods. Breads and muffins, for example, freeze well, as do chicken drumsticks. Put a frozen muffin in your child's lunch and it should have thawed by lunchtime. Using frozen bread will help keep your child's sandwich fresh.

On-the-Way-Home Noshing

If your child is like many, he probably gets hungry after school. If he can't wait to get home and have a snack, he may dip into his lunch box for a bite to eat. Unfortunately, even the best-protected lunch may no longer be safe to eat at three o'clock. Try to educate your child about which foods are safe to eat at the end of the day. (A peanut butter sandwich should be fine, for example, while an egg salad sandwich could be risky.) You might also pack something especially for after school, like some crackers or a bag of GORP (see page 112), or an orange.

But frozen bread or a frozen muffin isn't enough to keep an entire lunch box cold.

Use a good thermos. Test your child's thermos to make sure it keeps his drinks cold (or hot). Some thermoses that come with children's lunch boxes aren't as effective as they should be. Use a wide-mouthed thermos to pack salads and other foods that you want to keep cold.

Precool your child's thermos. Keep his thermos in the freezer overnight or rinse it with ice-cold water before filling it.

You can also keep food fresh by keeping it hot. For hot drinks or hot meals (like the Chili and Rice on page 78), use a conventional or wide-mouthed thermos. (Preheat the thermos by rinsing it with boiling water.) Make sure the food or drink you pour into the thermos is piping hot.

When you're packing both hot and cold foods in your child's lunch box, insulate them from one another. For example, if you're sending Hot Spiced Apple Juice (page 87), crackers, and a salad, pack the crackers between the hot thermos and the cold one. Or use a thick piece of cardboard as a divider.

Another way of ensuring that foods don't spoil is by using prepackaged foods, such as individually packaged applesauce or individual cans of fruit salad (see page 108).

Note: Certain foods are especially vulnerable to bacteria. Be very careful when packing foods containing meat, poultry, eggs, milk, and cream cheese.

Squish Prevention Strategies

• • •

I can well remember the feeling of opening my lunch box to find a squishy mess inside. My sandwich would be smushed flat and then curled back on itself, the peanut butter from my peanut butter and celery would be smeared all over its plastic wrap, and my plum would be a pulpy mess!

Making sure your child's lunch doesn't get mashed into a pulp will help to ensure that he eats it. Here's what you can do to prevent squish:

Use plastic containers. Manufacturers have created containers in practically every shape and size. There's a sandwich-size container as well as containers that are just right for salads, bite-size snacks, fruits, and other goodies. The challenge here is to persuade your child to remember to bring the containers home and not throw them away with the uneaten part of his lunch.

Use firm ingredients. A peach is more likely to squish than an orange. By the same token, a sandwich made of Wonder Bread is a lot more likely to squish than one made of a pita pocket or a hero roll. Use the anti-sog strategies suggested on page 50.

Wrap fruits and vegetables carefully. If you send a plum or other squishy food in your child's lunch, wrap it in several layers of paper towels and then put it in a plastic bag. Wrap cut vegetables in damp paper towels to keep them from drying out.

Recycled Containers

You don't have to buy plastic containers for your child's lunch. Just save the containers from the products listed below. After you wash them thoroughly, you can use them to pack your child's lunch. He can either bring them home to be used again or throw them out after lunch.

- Cottage cheese
- Yogurt
- Sour cream
- Cream cheese
- Peanut butter
- Dip
- Ricotta cheese
- Soft margarine

Note: Don't send glass containers—they could break. Never use containers from medicine, other pharmaceutical products, or cleaning products.

Pack the lunch box strategically. When your child's lunch box is open on the counter, pack it from the bottom up. Put in his thermos and any plastic containers first and then layer the remaining food upward, with the heaviest foods on the bottom. Use a couple of napkins to fill in any blank spaces. The less empty space you have in the box, the better.

4

Add Some Fun

Riddles to Go

Send your child a riddle in her lunch and she'll have something to laugh about and share with her friends. In case you're feeling uninspired one morning, here are some grade-school winners.

Q. What's round and red and goes up and down?
A. A tomato in an elevator.

Q. What's black and white and green and black and white?
A. Two zebras fighting over a pickle.

Q. What kind of room has no walls, no floor, and no ceiling?
A. A mushroom.

You can make your child's lunch really special by packing in a few extras. You certainly don't have to do this kind of thing every day, but once in a while, finding something extra in her lunch box is a nice treat for your child.

Here are some of the ways you can make your child's lunch more inviting:

Tie it with a bow. After you've wrapped your child's sandwich in plastic, gift-wrap it! Or wrap it in the colored plastic wraps that are now available. This is a nice idea for birthdays or other special occasions.

Stickers. Use colorful stickers to seal the plastic wrap on your child's sandwich and other foods. You might also want to pack a few stickers in your child's lunch as a present.

Save those condiments. Next time you're at a fast food restaurant, save your unopened packages of ketchup, mustard, pepper, and so on. As needed, you can pack them in your child's lunch.

Use colorful paper products. A colored paper napkin will brighten up your child's day. Around the holidays, pack seasonal napkins. You might also try a colorful paper plate or a paper doily to use as a placemat. A heart-shaped one would be perfect for Valentine's Day!

Send a little present. You could send your child a small gift, such as a new pencil or eraser or small figure of one of her favorite characters. Buy some packs of party favors and send them one at a time, as the spirit moves you.

Send a note. Most children like to get notes from home. Even a preschooler can understand this classic rebus:

Don't take this opportunity to remind your child to bring home her sweater or to practice her spelling words during recess. This is a time for a loving, friendly message. Caution: Your child may reach an age when she feels notes are "babyish." Make sure to respect her views on this matter.

Q. What do you get when you cross an insect and a rabbit?
A. Bugs Bunny.

Q. What has four wheels and flies?
A. A garbage truck.

Q. What do elephants have that no other animals have?
A. Baby elephants.

Q. Why is a spider a good baseball player?
A. Because it catches flies.

Labeling Your Child's Lunch

Child-protection experts advise against displaying your child's name on his clothing or other possessions. One friend of mine has written her son's name, address, and phone number on the *inside* of his lunch box so that if it gets lost it will be returned to him. To help him distinguish *his* He-Man lunch box from his classmates', she put a special sticker on the outside of his lunch box. By the same token, you might want to put your child's name inside his lunch bag or under the folded-over flap.

Pack fun utensils. Pack a collapsible cup or a crazy straw or a colorful plastic fork or spoon. To make a fun straw, write your child's name on a 3×3-inch square of construction paper. Punch holes at the top and bottom of this square and poke the straw through them.

Spencer

Pack an individually wrapped moistened towel. It makes cleanup elegant!

When is a Lunch Box Not a Lunch Box?

Your child may be tired of carrying a lunch box to school. If so, there are plenty of alternatives, including these:

- A small straw basket
- A small knapsack
- A fanny pack (which straps around the waist)
- A small, elegant shopping bag with handles
- A small cloth tote bag
- A large purse or shoulder bag

Brown Bagging It

On days when she has after-school activities, my daughter prefers to take her lunch to school in a bag so she doesn't have to tote her lunch box around all day. On those mornings, I take a paper bag and decorate it. Sometimes I make a picture I know she'll like—of unicorns in a field or a little house with children looking out the window and a rainbow overhead, and so on. Other times I make a maze or other activity she can do during lunch.

In addition to the conventional brown paper lunch bags, you can also buy insulated freezer bags, which keep food fresher.

Bag Critters

If your child likes to bring her lunch in a bag, you can make the bag more interesting by turning it into an animal. For example, draw elephant eyes and a mouth on a bag. Cut out ears and a trunk from another bag and tape them on.

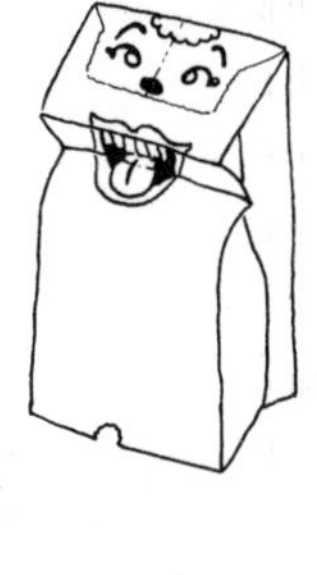

Or draw a face on the bottom of the bag, with the mouth overlapping onto the bag itself. When your child is done eating, she can entertain her friends with this puppet.

Where to Buy Lunch Boxes

Lunch boxes have come a long way since we were kids. You can still buy the traditional square metal or plastic lunch box with the licensed characters pasted on the outside. Or you can get a molded plastic lunch box shaped like a school bus, a cloth camouflage lunch box, a lunch box with a shoulder strap, or a hiker's backpack or fanny pack. Shop in children's specialty stores, department stores, and camping supply stores as well as drugstores, supermarkets, and toy stores. If you don't find what you want, you may be able to find it in one of these catalogs.

Just for Kids carries tons of stuff, including cloth lunch bags.
Phone: 800-654-6963

Childcraft features unusual plastic lunch boxes.
Phone: 800-631-5657

L.L. Bean offers fanny packs as well as other sporty gear.
Phone: 800–341-4341

Recipes

5

Sandwiches

Believe it or not, the first sandwich was not consumed at a modern American school cafeteria. It was eaten at a gambling table in eighteenth-century England. As the story goes, John Montagu, the fourth Earl of Sandwich, was reluctant to leave his game for a proper meal, so he asked for a piece of meat between two hunks of bread. This wasn't the first time such a meal had been consumed, but it was the first time this humble repast was given a name. Ever since, a grateful public has honored the earl's ingenuity by calling sandwiches after him.

Today the sandwich is the meal of choice for most school lunches. A sandwich is one of the most efficient ways to make sure your child gets food from at least two of the basic food groups—grain and protein. In many cases you can slip in some dairy products and fruits and vegetables as well.

The sandwich has another advantage, one that the earl appreciated over two centuries ago. It's easy to eat and can be consumed quickly. For kids who are impatient to get out to the playground, a sandwich is the ideal main course.

Unfortunately, most sandwiches don't freeze especially well. You can make sandwiches the night before, although they're apt to get soggy (see Anti-Sog Strategies on page 50). If your mornings are rushed (and whose aren't these days?), it will help if you get the ingredients together the night before. Mix up your egg or tuna salad, for example, or have a slice of turkey and a slice of cheese and a bagel ready to go. Then you can just assemble the sandwich before everyone leaves for the day.

Peanut Butter and . . .

You say your child has been going to school every day for the last three years with a peanut butter and jelly sandwich in her lunch box? Relax—she could do a lot worse. The peanuts in peanut butter are protein-rich, especially when paired with bread. Do check the label when you shop, however, and bring home only salt- and sugar-free peanut butter. As for the jelly, you're in luck. The new fruit-only jellies and jams provide a healthful alternative to sugar-laced varieties. In addition to the classic, unadulterated PB&J sandwich, try to get your child to sample some of these tasty varieties.

2 tablespoons peanut butter

1 to 3 teaspoons any of the following: canned crushed pineapple (choose the kind packed in its own juice), applesauce, mashed or sliced banana, flavored yogurt, raisins, diced dates, grated carrot, diced apple

2 slices bread

If you're adding pineapple, applesauce, flavored yogurt, mashed banana, or grated carrots, mash up the peanut butter in a small bowl and then mix in the extra ingredients before spreading the peanut butter mixture on the bread. If you're adding sliced banana, raisins, dates, or diced apple, you can simply spread two slices of bread with peanut butter, sprinkle the extra ingredients on the peanut butter, and then close the sandwich.

About Bread

Any way you slice it, bread is a key ingredient in most lunch box meals, especially if you're packing a sandwich. Breads made from whole wheat (or other whole grains) have greater nutritional value than does white bread, because they're made of flour that includes the germ and the bran, which are milled out of white flour. Read the label carefully; just because a bread has a darker color doesn't mean it's actually made of whole grain. If your child insists on white bread only, make sure to buy a brand that has been made with enriched flour.

Cutout Cut-Ups

Your child will get a kick out of lunch when you send him to school with little sandwiches shaped in hearts, stars, bells, and other forms. Just get out your cookie cutters and, once the sandwich is made, cut out his favorite shapes. Toward Christmas, you could use Christmas trees, Santa, and angel cookie cutters. Your child probably won't mind if you pile in the odd, leftover shapes the cookie cutters leave behind.

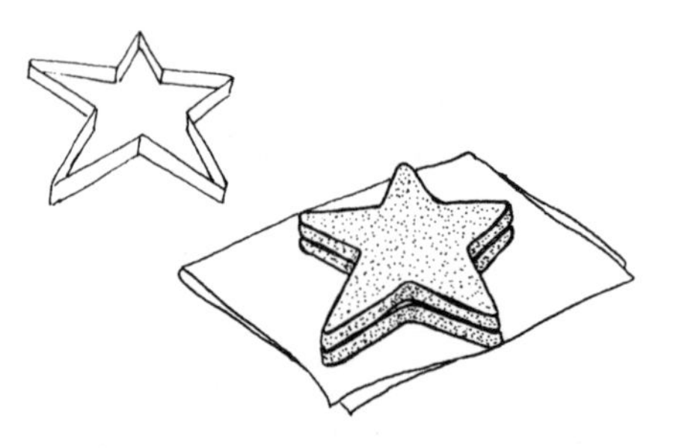

Cream Cheese and . . .

Cream cheese tastes great, spreads nicely, and mixes well with other ingredients. Unfortunately, cream cheese is somewhat less nutritious than other cheeses, owing to its relatively high fat content and relatively low protein content. If your child will go for it, you might try substituting cottage cheese, farmer's cheese, or feta cheese (or mix them with cream cheese). Or mix in a little powdered milk to give the cream cheese a protein boost. In any case, you can beef up cream cheese by adding some of the ingredients listed below.

2 tablespoons cream cheese
1 to 3 teaspoons any of the following: chopped walnuts, pecans, almonds, or other nuts; grated carrot; diced cucumber, green and/or red pepper, or celery; diced orange, apple, or pear; raisins; chopped dates; minced clams
2 slices bread

In a small bowl, mix the cream cheese with a fork until it's creamy. You might add a few drops of milk to help this process along. Then mix in the additional ingredients. Smooth this paste onto two slices of bread and fit them together. A cream cheese sandwich holds together nicely, so you might want to cut the sandwich into interesting shapes.

Tuna Fish and . . .

Tuna fish is an old standby and a good one. It provides one of the few sources of fish most kids will eat. Choose the water-packed variety rather than the kind that is saturated in oil. Whether served plain or dressed up with some of the additional ingredients listed below, a tuna fish sandwich is a healthful treat.

1 can tuna fish
Mayonnaise and/or plain yogurt to taste
Any of the following additional ingredients: grated carrots; diced celery, cucumber, green or red pepper; minced onion; pickle relish or diced pickle; chopped egg; alfalfa sprouts
Margarine or mayonnaise
2 slices bread
Lettuce leaf

Empty the can of tuna into a small bowl. Mix in just enough mayonnaise and/or yogurt to bind the tuna. Add as many of the additional ingredients as you think your child will enjoy. Spread a thin layer of margarine or mayonnaise on two slices of bread. Pile on the tuna and a leaf of lettuce and close the sandwich. Since you will have enough tuna salad for more than one sandwich, store leftovers in an airtight container in the refrigerator.

Note: This recipe works well with crabmeat and salmon too.

Another approach is to use the cookie cutter but leave the shape inside the frame of bread. You can also use cookie cutters on cheese or lunch meat. Take a slice of cheese and cut out a shape. Now layer a sandwich like this: bread, cutout cheese shape, meat, cheese silhouette, bread.

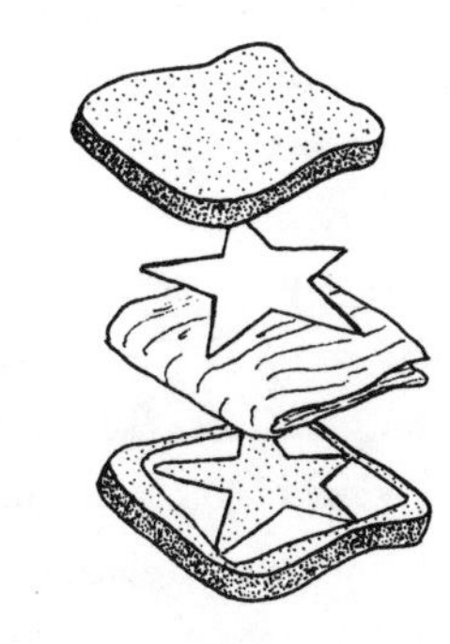

***Note:* On Valentine's Day, make sure to use your heart-shaped cookie cutter!**

The Good News and the Bad News About Mayonnaise

Never pack homemade mayonnaise in your child's lunch. It spoils rapidly and may contain salmonella bacteria. The good news about commercial mayonnaise, however, is that it is prepared with antispoilage additives and is safe to use in a lunch box with an ice pack or other coolant.

The bad news is that mayonnaise is full of fat. You can reduce the fat content of your child's salad or sandwich by substituting yogurt for all or part of the mayonnaise and by keeping the mayonnaise content of the sandwich to a reasonable minimum. Or use lowfat mayonnaise.

Chicken Salad Sandwich

The classic chicken salad sandwich is made with chunks of chicken and mayonnaise or yogurt, and it tastes wonderful. Adding some of the ingredients listed below will give it some extra crunch and flavor as well as extra vitamins. This is a great way to use up leftover chicken.

3 tablespoons diced, cooked chicken

1 teaspoon mayonnaise and/or plain yogurt

1 to 2 teaspoons any of the following: chopped walnuts, pecans, almonds, or peanuts; chopped pickle; grated cheese; diced celery, cucumber, green or red pepper; sliced mushrooms; grated carrots

Margarine or mayonnaise

2 slices bread

In a small bowl, mix the cooked chicken with the mayonnaise and/or yogurt. Stir in the additional ingredients. You may find you need more mayonnaise and/or yogurt, but start with just a little and work up to the right proportions. Spread each piece of bread with a very thin layer of margarine or mayonnaise. Fill the sandwich with the chicken salad mixture.

Tropical Ham Sandwich

• • •

If your child is up for something a little more exotic than ham and cheese, he'll probably enjoy this unusual sandwich. There's enough sweet, yummy fruit here to whet his appetite to give this sandwich a try. Since there's plenty of fruit in this sandwich, you can keep the ham down to a minimum, if you want.

Margarine
2 slices toast
1/4 banana
1 slice pineapple
1 to 4 pieces ham, thinly sliced
1 slice orange (peel removed)

Spread a very thin layer of margarine on one slice of toast. Mash the banana and spread it on the other slice. Wipe the pineapple slice dry with a paper towel. Place the ham, pineapple, and orange on the slice with the margarine. Close the sandwich. Depending on how much you've packed into the sandwich, you might want to cut it into quarters and use a toothpick to hold each quarter together.

The Kindest Cut

Most kids love novelty, a quality that can be all too lacking in lunch box fare, especially if your child is an adamant fan of just one type of sandwich. One way to liven up a lunch is to cut your child's sandwich differently. Here are some possibilities:

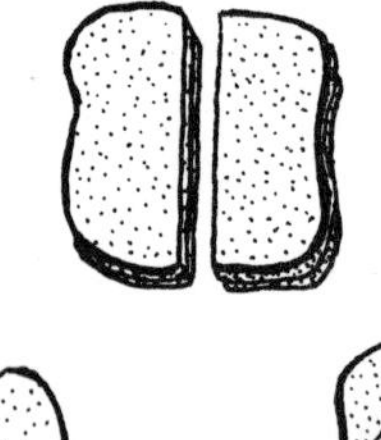

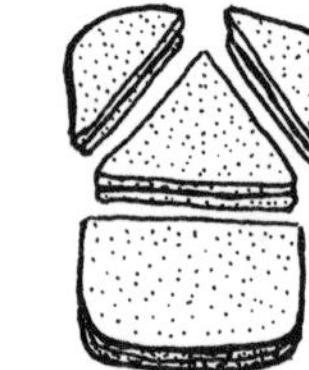

Bagels and Lox

Here's a great way to slip some fish into your child's diet. Lox by any other name is smoked salmon. Where I live, in New York City, lox is available at practically any corner market. But if lox isn't a staple in your community, you can probably buy it at a fish store. Or you can buy canned salmon and mix it with cream cheese to form a paste.

1 bagel
2 tablespoons cream cheese
1 slice lox

Optional extras: 1 slice tomato, 1 slice Bermuda onion, 1 teaspoon capers

Cut the bagel in half and spread the cream cheese on each half. Place the lox (and the optional extras—if your child is a *serious* bagel and lox eater) on top of one bagel/cream cheese half and cover it with the other half of the bagel.

Avocado and . . .

If your child loves avocado, you've probably served it to him on salads or as a guacamole dip. But have you ever thought of sending him to school with an avocado sandwich? Avocados are nutritious—they contain eleven different vitamins. Avocado meat turns brown quickly once the fruit it opened, so I've included a little lemon juice in this recipe to help the sandwich spread retain that pleasing light-green color. Instead of the spreadable avocado recipe I've given, you may want to simply place thinly sliced strips of avocado (sprinkled with lemon juice) on your child's sandwich, perhaps in combination with lunch meat or other ingredients. To decide whether an avocado is ripe enough to use, squeeze it gently with your whole hand. If it feels slightly squishy, it's ready to eat.

1/4 ripe, peeled avocado
1/4 teaspoon lemon juice
Any of the following: 1 teaspoon imitation bacon bits; 2 teaspoons chopped walnuts, pecans, almonds, or other nuts; 1 teaspoon chopped tomato pulp; 1 to 2 teaspoons wheat germ; 1 to 2 tablespoons shredded chicken or other meat; 1 to 2 tablespoons sesame or sunflower seeds
2 slices toast

Put the avocado in a small bowl and mash it with the back of a fork. Blend in the lemon juice. Mix in the other ingredients and spread the mixture on toast. Fit the sandwich together and wrap it tightly. The avocado will stay fresher if you send it in an airtight container and in a lunch box with a freezer pack.

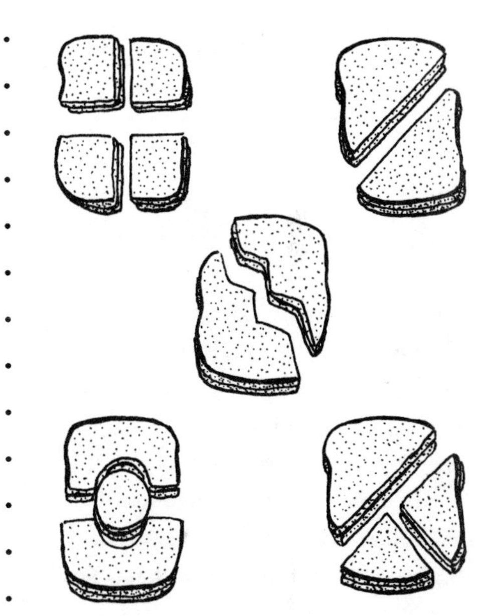

Make Your Own Lunch Meat

Prepackaged lunch meats have long been a staple of American lunch box fare. But too frequently these meats are processed with excessive amounts of nitrates, nitrites, sodium, and other additives. They may also contain a good deal of fat. Try to limit your use of these meats and load up your child's meat sandwich with vegetables and other healthful ingredients. Look for lunch meats that are low in fat. You can also make your own.

Practically the best sandwich meat is chicken. And one of the easiest ways to get plenty of great chicken meat is to poach boneless chicken breasts. Just put the chicken breasts into a saucepan or deep frying pan and cover them with

The Dagwood Sandwich

Just as there are meat-and-potatoes people, so there are people (kids included) for whom a sandwich isn't a sandwich unless it's piled high with slices of lunch meat, cheese, and other goodies. You may be able to persuade your meat-and-cheese guy or gal to throw on some lettuce and other vegetables as well. Why not put out the ingredients and let your child put the sandwich together any way he wants?

A hero roll

Sandwich meat—turkey, chicken, ham, roast beef, etc.

Sliced cheese—Swiss, Muenster, Cheddar, etc.

Any of these extras: lettuce, spinach, or watercress; sliced mushrooms; sliced olives; alfalfa or bean sprouts; sliced tomato; sliced onion; capers; artichoke hearts; sliced beets

Any of these condiments: margarine, mayonnaise, mustard, ketchup, pickle relish, chutney, taco sauce

See which of these ingredients you have in your kitchen and then offer your child his choice.

Super-Hero Sandwich

• • •

Here's a super sandwich for the kid who can't sit still to eat an elaborate meal. There's plenty of protein for your high-energy child and a special feature that tells him you think he's special.

Lettuce

Sliced Swiss, Muenster, or Cheddar cheese

Lunch meat (homemade or store-bought)

Hero roll

Mustard, liquid margarine, or ketchup (in a squeeze bottle)

Put the lettuce, your child's favorite cheese, and a layer of lunch meat on the hero roll. Now, using a squeeze bottle of mustard, liquid margarine, or ketchup (depending on your child's taste), write the first initial of his name in a bold letter (à la Superman's *S*). If he's interested, you might ask him to make the letter himself. Close the sandwich. Wrap the finished product tightly—the letter will still be there when your child eats the sandwich at lunchtime.

cold water. Put them over a low flame and bring them to a gentle simmer. Continue cooking for 10 to 15 minutes. Check to make sure they're done by cutting into them. There should be no trace of pink, but the meat should still be moist and springy to the touch. Cut thin strips for sandwiches. (This is also a handy way to produce cold cooked chicken for chicken salad.)

Many supermarkets now carry chicken cutlets, which are even easier to use than chicken breasts. These thin strips of chicken breast can be poached or sautéed for just a few minutes (2 to 5 minutes on each side if sautéing, 5 to 10 minutes if poaching) and are ready to serve on a sandwich.

For other kinds of lunch meat, you can cook a big roast for your family's dinner and slice off pieces for sandwiches.

Mini-Sub

Small children often find it difficult to manage a grown-up–size hero roll. For a mini-sub sandwich, use a hot dog roll instead. Or check your bread or deli counter for mini-sub rolls.

Fruit Sandwich

This tasty sandwich has a little of everything—bread, fruit, a dairy product, and a source of extra protein. Plus it's got plenty of crunch and tastes great.

3 tablespoons small-curd cottage cheese
2 tablespoons chopped apple or pear or dried apricot
2 tablespoons slivered almonds
2 tablespoons crushed pineapple (in natural juice)
2 slices bread

In a small bowl, mix all the ingredients (except the bread) together. You may need to add a little more cottage cheese to bind the ingredients. Spread the mixture on the bread. This sandwich is especially good when served on some of the quick breads you'll find recipes for in Chapter 9.

Egg Salad Sandwich

Eggs spoil easily, so if your child wants an egg salad sandwich for lunch, pack it in a lunch box with a freezer pack. Eggs are a great source of protein, but the yolks are just about the most potent source of cholesterol going (see page 17). If your child just loves egg salad and wants it frequently, you might try using only half the egg yolk and the entire cholesterol-free egg white for each sandwich.

1 hard-boiled egg

1 teaspoon mayonnaise and/or plain yogurt

Any of these additional ingredients: 1/4 teaspoon mustard; 1 tablespoon shredded chicken, ham, or other meat; 1 tablespoon mashed avocado; 1 teaspoon minced onion; 1 to 2 teaspoons diced celery, carrot, cucumber, mushroom, red or green pepper, or tomato; 1/2 teaspoon pickle relish; 1 lettuce or spinach leaf

2 slices toast or thick bread

To hard-boil an egg, gently place it in a pot of cold water. Bring the water to a boil and keep it boiling 10 to 15 minutes. Pour out the boiling water and run cold water on the egg for a minute or two. Leave the egg sitting in the cold water until it's cold too. Peel it under cold running water.

Separate the yolk from the egg white. Mash the yolk in a small bowl with the mayonnaise and/or yogurt, adding more mayo and/or yogurt if needed. Chop up the egg white. Mix it and any of the additional ingredients (except the lettuce or spinach) into the egg yolk mixture. Spread the egg salad on toast or thick bread. If you like, add a lettuce or spinach leaf before closing the sandwich.

Mix 'n' Match

What do you do if your child can't decide between egg salad and tuna fish? Send both! Pep up your child's lunch with an assortment of sandwiches. This strategy works especially well if you have two or more children. Just make two or more sandwiches, cut them in half (or in thirds or quarters) and send each child to school with a variety pack. If you have only one child, make smaller portions of sandwich spread (or other ingredients) and use one slice of bread cut in half for each sandwich half. Another way to vary the meal is to use two different kinds of bread for one sandwich.

Beyond Bread

There's more than one way to make a sandwich. Conventional sliced bread is just the beginning. Here are some alternatives:

- **Toasted English muffin**
- **Biscuits**
- **Croissant**
- **Matzos**
- **Pita Bread**
- **Bagel**
- **Rice cake**
- **Crackers**
- **Muffins and quick bread (see Chapter 9)**
- **Hamburger or hot dog buns**
- **Tortilla**

Note: **Try to find products that are made with whole grains. If whole grain isn't available, look for products made with enriched flour.**

Banana-Wich

Bananas are loaded with potassium and other good nutrients, and their naturally sweet taste makes them a winner with most kids. Here's a sandwich that's bound to please even a finicky eater. The additional ingredients add protein to the sandwich. Bananas ripen quickly at home, so buy them when they're not quite ready and let them ripen on your kitchen shelf.

1/2 banana
A few drops milk (optional)
2 teaspoons any of these additional ingredients: wheat germ; chopped walnuts, pecans, almonds, or other nuts; sesame or sunflower seeds
2 slices bread

In a small bowl, mash the banana with the back of a fork. You may want to add a few drops of milk to make the banana creamier. Stir in as many of the additional ingredients as you think your child will like. Spread the banana mixture on a slice of bread and top with the other slice of bread. Another way to make a banana sandwich is simply to slice the banana and layer the banana rounds between two slices of bread that have been thinly spread with margarine.

Chicken Taco

If your child likes Mexican food, he's sure to go for this dish. The tortilla provides a nice change of pace from bread, and it's fun to eat a rolled-up sandwich.

1 teaspoon margarine
1 corn or flour tortilla
1 to 2 teaspoons mild taco sauce
4 tablespoons shredded chicken
2 tablespoons shredded cheese
2 tablespoons shredded lettuce

Heat the margarine in a frying pan and quickly sauté the tortilla (about a minute on each side). Place the tortilla on a piece of waxed paper. Spread the taco sauce on the tortilla. Sprinkle the chicken, cheese, and lettuce on one third of the tortilla. Then roll the tortilla up, starting with the side where the chicken mixture is and folding the ends in to prevent the mixture from dripping out. Wrap the waxed paper around the taco and pack it in a plastic bag.

In Praise of Lettuce

A leaf or two of lettuce enhances any sandwich and adds vitamins too. On the whole, the dark-green or reddish-green lettuce leaves pack the most nutritional punch. So steer clear of iceberg—unless it's the only kind your kid will eat—and lean toward romaine and red-leaf lettuce. If your child will eat them, spinach and watercress make wonderful substitutes for lettuce. Or try alfalfa sprouts. If you think your child will go to the trouble, you could pack the lettuce leaves separately so that they stay crisp all morning. Then he can pack them into the sandwich when he's ready to eat.

Anti-Sog Strategies

Has your child ever left the house with a fresh, beautiful sandwich in his lunch box only to find a soggy mess when he opens his lunch at the school cafeteria? Here are some strategies that will reduce sog:

• ***Use a sandwich spread on both pieces of bread.*** This can be margarine, mayonnaise, peanut butter, or whatever spreadable mixture you're using on the day's sandwich. If you're using margarine or mayonnaise, spread it thinly, but spread right to the edges of the bread where it can form a protective barrier between the bread and the filling.

• ***Make sure you use dry ingredients.*** It's important to wash lettuce and other

Pocket Pizza

Most kids would eat pizza five times a week if they had the chance. Here's a recipe for a sandwich that uses the same ingredients as pizza. The pita bread approximates the texture of a pizza crust. And all your child's other favorite flavors are there too. It isn't hot but it is yummy.

1 pocket pita bread
1 to 2 teaspoons pizza or spaghetti sauce
2 tablespoons mozzarella cheese
2 tablespoons toppings: chopped green pepper, chopped onion, anchovies, chopped olives, sliced salami

Cut a slit in the top third of the pita pocket. Spread pizza or spaghetti sauce all around inside the pita. Add mozzarella cheese and your child's favorite pizza topping(s).

Sandwich Roll-Ups

• • •

Here's something different. These pinwheels of bread and filling look great and they're fun to eat. Let your child help make them!

1 slice soft bread
Spreadable sandwich mixture (see Peanut Butter and . . ., page 37; Cream Cheese and . . ., page 38; or Egg Salad Sandwich, page 46)

Place the bread between two sheets of waxed paper. Gently roll the bread out with a rolling pin until it is flat and firm, then peel away the waxed paper. Now spoon on enough sandwich spread to cover the bread in a thin layer. Starting at one end, begin rolling up the bread as you would a jelly roll, being careful to pinch the ingredients together as you roll. Wrap the roll in plastic and refrigerate for at least one hour (or overnight). Then cut ½-inch slices to form perfect pinwheel shapes. Skewer the slices with festive toothpicks.

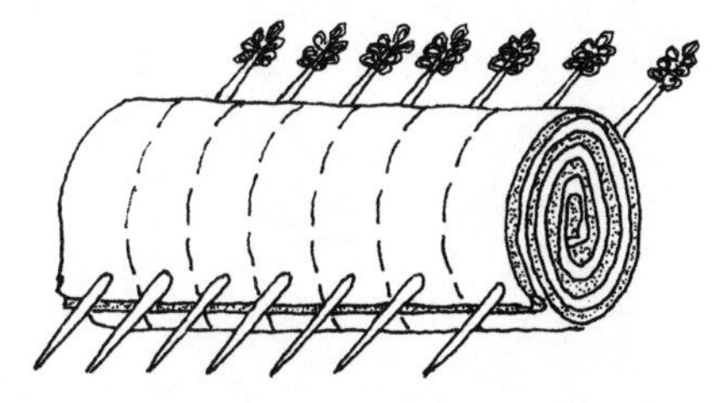

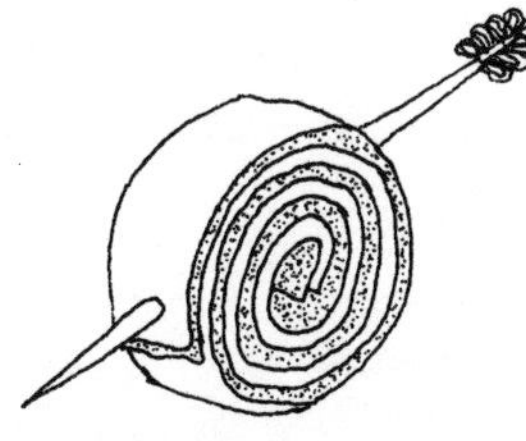

ingredients, but dry them before putting them in the sandwich.

• *Store your bread in the freezer.* Take out two slices in the morning and make a sandwich. The bread will thaw by lunchtime, but it's less likely to absorb its filling when it's frozen.

• *Toast the bread.* Bread that is evenly and lightly toasted holds a gloppy mixture more securely than regular bread.

• *Use thick rolls or hamburger buns.* Even if some of the filling seeps in, a roll or bun is likely to hold up.

• *Pack soggy ingredients separately.* A slice of tomato, for example, is almost guaranteed to seep into the bread. Pack the tomato separately and let your child add it to his sandwich. Or layer the tomato (or other soggy ingredient) between sturdier ingredients.

Cheese, Please!

Like any milk product, cheese is rich in calcium, phosphorus, protein, and various vitamins. If your child won't drink milk, cheese is a great alternative. An ounce and a half of hard cheese provides the nutritional equivalent of a cup of milk!

Cheese can also be rich in fats and cholesterol (see Fats and Cholesterol on pages 16 and 17). The cheeses that are lowest in fats and cholesterol are cottage cheese, ricotta cheese, mozzarella, feta, and farmer's cheese. Natural

Apple and Cheese Sandwich

This satisfying alternative to routine sandwich fare contains two of kids' favorite foods—apples and cheese. In season, you might want to substitute pears for the apples. Though the cheese provides some protein, it's a good idea to pack another protein source, such as a chicken leg (page 108) or some Peanut Butter Balls (page 107).

1/4 to 1/2 apple
A few drops lemon juice
Either 2 to 3 tablespoons ricotta or farmer's cheese or 1 to 2 slices Muenster, Swiss, Cheddar, or other favorite cheese
Margarine
2 slices bread

After slicing the apple thinly, sprinkle the slices with lemon juice to keep them from turning brown. If you're using ricotta or farmer's cheese, spread margarine thinly on one slice of bread. Coat the other slice with the cheese, pile on the apple slices, and close the sandwich. If you're using sliced cheese, spread a thin layer of margarine on both slices of bread, then layer slices of cheese and slices of apple, and close the sandwich.

Week-After-Thanksgiving Sandwich

• • •

Ever since I was little and my mother sent me to school with this sandwich at the end of every November, this has been my favorite meal in the world. I like it much better than the complete soup-to-nuts holiday meal. The fact that the ingredients are only on hand once a year makes it even yummier!

2 slices bread
1 to 2 teaspoons cranberry sauce
1 to 3 slices turkey
2 to 3 tablespoons stuffing

Spread two slices of bread with cranberry sauce. Spread one side with stuffing and top with the turkey. Close the sandwich. If there's any left over from Thanksgiving dinner, I make this sandwich on cranberry bread. Heavenly!

cheeses, such as Swiss, Cheddar, Muenster, and Parmesan, contain more fats and cholesterol but are still good choices as long as they don't become the main staple of your child's diet. Processed cheeses—such as American cheese—and packaged cheese "spreads" contain a variety of food additives and in some cases additional fats.

Don't limit your use of cheese to sandwiches. Send some cheese along as a course in itself. Cut hard cheese into interesting shapes (hearts, stars, houses, and so on) or send farmer's or feta cheese in its own little container. Send along some crackers too!

6

Salads

Although sandwiches are the leaders in lunch box fare, salads make a nice change of pace. You can send a salad as a main course, a side dish, or a dessert.

The main challenge in sending a salad to school is keeping it from getting wilted and soggy by the time your child is ready for lunch. In some cases, I've recommended sending the salad dressing and/or some of the more perishable ingredients separate from the rest of the salad. You may also want to look back at the tuna, egg, and chicken salads suggested as sandwich fillings—these all stand up well by themselves.

With the salad, you should send along some bread, a muffin, or some crackers as well as another protein source (if needed) and a dairy product (again, as needed).

Unless otherwise indicated, each of the salads on these pages is designed to make a single 1-cup serving.

Pasta-Tuna Salad

Make enough of this tasty salad for your own lunch too. You can use whatever kind of pasta your child likes best. Shells work particularly well, since the tuna fills up the shells when you toss the salad.

4 tablespoons mayonnaise and/or plain yogurt
1/2 teaspoon lemon juice
1/2 teaspoon dried parsley
1 small (6 1/2-ounce) can tuna (packed in water)
2 tablespoons minced onion
2 tablespoons minced celery and/or cucumber
2 tablespoons diced green or red pepper
2 tablespoons grated carrot
2 cups cooked pasta

In a medium-size bowl, combine the mayonnaise and/or yogurt, lemon juice, and parsley to make a dressing. Drain the tuna fish. Add the tuna and vegetables to the dressing. Add the pasta and toss until the salad is well blended. Put it in lunch box containers and refrigerate overnight.

Yield: About three 1-cup servings

Pocket Salad

Here's a salad that's easy to manage and doesn't require a fork! Team it up with some additional protein—like a chicken drumstick—and some juice, and you'll have a well-balanced meal!

1 pocket pita bread
2 tablespoons grated carrot
2 tablespoons grated cheese
1 tablespoon chopped celery, green pepper, or red cabbage
1 tablespoon chopped tomatoes
1 tablespoon Yogurt-Honey or Cucumber dressings (see pages 73 to 74)

Make a slit in the top third of the pita bread. Fill the pocket with the carrot, cheese, and celery, green pepper, or red cabbage. Wrap the pocket in plastic wrap. In separate containers, pack the chopped tomatoes and the dressing. When your child gets to the cafeteria, she can add the tomatoes and the dressing. (Otherwise they might make the salad soggy.)

Fruity Rice Salad

The rice and sunflower seeds in this recipe combine to make a good source of protein. And the fruit offers plenty of vitamins. If your child doesn't think it's "yucky," use brown rice. Protein, vitamins, and minerals are all diminished when brown rice is processed into white.

1/2 cup cooked and cooled rice
1/2 teaspoon vegetable oil
1/4 cup crushed pineapple (in natural juice)
1/2 orange
2 tablespoons sunflower seeds

Put the rice in a medium-size bowl and toss it with the vegetable oil. Add the pineapple with enough juice to form a light coating on the rice. Divide the orange half into sections and cut each section into thirds. Add the orange pieces and the sunflower seeds and mix all the ingredients together. Make the night before and refrigerate the salad in its lunch box container.

Yogurt and Fruit

Commercial yogurt with mixed-in fruit is a good choice for your child's lunch box. Even better, though, is plain or vanilla yogurt with fresh fruit. At home, you can regulate the amount of sweetener that goes into the yogurt, and you can send a more generous portion of fruit than usually comes in the store-bought variety.

4 to 6 ounces plain or vanilla yogurt

1/4 to 1/2 cup any combination of the following: chopped apple, pear, peach, nectarine, melon, plum, or papaya; sliced banana; crushed or chunked pineapple; whole blueberries or raspberries, sliced strawberries; sectioned and sliced orange or tangerine; wheat germ; chopped nuts; sesame and/or sunflower seeds; honey or sugar to taste (optional)

This salad is best when made in the morning right before school, so that the fruit stays as fresh as possible. Store the fruit and the yogurt in the refrigerator overnight, so all the ingredients will be cold when they leave the house. To prepare, put the yogurt in a wide-mouth thermos or a lunch box container. Mix in the fruit and other ingredients.

Halloween Cucumber Monster

Here's a scary surprise for your child's Halloween lunch box. Take a small cucumber (or use a pickle) and carve out a frightening mouth and tail, as illustrated. Use a vegetable peeler to scrape some fin shapes. Scoop out eye sockets. Now take pieces of red pepper and attach eyes and tongue with cream cheese. Aaaaaggggghhhh!

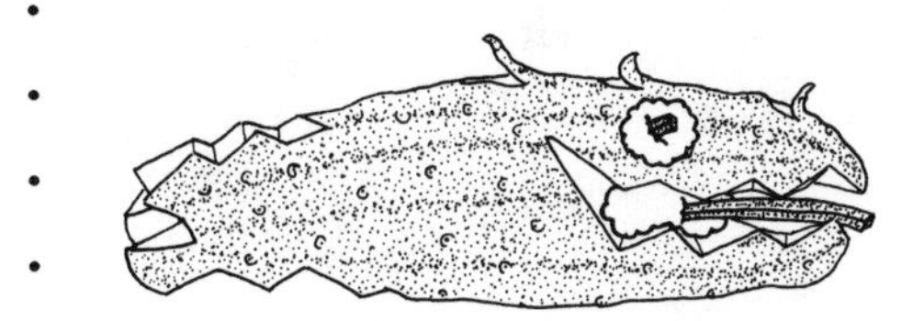

Waldorf Salad

This tasty salad gets its name from the glamorous Waldorf-Astoria hotel in New York, where it was reportedly invented. From these elite origins, it has become a favorite dish in homes around the country. If you add meat, the salad becomes a main course in itself—you just need to send some bread and milk along to complete the picture. (Or, if you want to make this a main dish but don't want to use meat, add more nuts and some sunflower seeds.)

1/2 apple
A few drops lemon juice
1/2 orange
2 tablespoons chopped celery
2 tablespoons chopped walnuts
1/4 cup cubed, cooked chicken or ham (optional)
Yogurt-Honey Dressing (page 73)

Core and chop the apple (leaving on the skin) and put it into a small bowl. Sprinkle on the lemon juice and toss. (The lemon juice helps keep the apple from turning brown.) Separate the orange into sections and cut each section into thirds. Add the orange and the rest of the ingredients except the dressing to the apple. Toss the salad. Pour on the dressing, a little at a time, and toss again. This salad won't hold up very well overnight—it's better to keep all the ingredients in the fridge and assemble the salad in the morning.

Oriental Chicken Salad

I never tasted Chinese food until I was well into my teens. My daughter, however, has been eating Chinese food since she was a year old. Egg rolls, *mu shu* pork, and boiled dumplings are part of many American children's culinary vocabularies. Here's a salad that draws on Chinese and other Oriental recipes. You can vary the ingredients according to your child's taste.

1 small (8-ounce) can crushed pineapple (in natural juice)
4 ounces (half an 8-ounce can) sliced water chestnuts
1 cup cooked, cubed chicken
2 tablespoons sliced green onion
Oriental Dressing *(page 75)*

Drain the pineapple. Cut the sliced water chestnuts into smaller slivers. Put all the ingredients except the dressing into a small bowl and lightly toss. Pour on the dressing, a little at a time, and toss until the salad ingredients are coated with the dressing. Refrigerate the salad overnight in its lunch box container.

Yield: Two to three 1-cup servings

Orange Boats

Here's a fun way to send a salad to school. Take a pencil and trace a design around the top third of an orange. Then, with a sharp knife, cut into the orange along the pencil line. Gently pull the orange apart and scoop out the orange sections. Use them in a salad, such as Citrus Chicken Salad (page 62) or Waldorf Salad (page 60). Now fill the larger orange peel section with the salad. Fit the top back on and wrap the orange tightly in plastic wrap. At school, your child will open what looks like an orange and find a salad boat instead. Send along a toothpick flag for a sail.

Citrus Chicken Salad

The recipe for chicken salad in the sandwich section of this book (page 40) makes a nice meal without bread too. Here's a tasty alternative that adds citrus fruit to the menu.

1/2 orange or 1/3 grapefruit
1/2 cup cooked, cubed chicken
2 tablespoons chopped walnuts
Citrus Dressing (page 74)

Divide the orange or grapefruit into sections and cut the sections into bite-size pieces. In a small bowl, toss together the chicken, the fruit, and the nuts. Add the citrus dressing. Toss and refrigerate the salad overnight in its lunch box container.

Jolly Good Gelatin

Most kids love Jell-O. This recipe is just as easy to make and lets you make sure that your child has a healthful, sugar-free treat. Load the gelatin up with fruit and you've got a wholesome salad!

1 packet unflavored gelatin
1 cup grape or apple juice concentrate, thawed
1 cup boiling water
Sliced or diced fruit: banana, apple, strawberry, peach, grapes, melon, etc.

In a medium-size bowl, sprinkle the gelatin onto the concentrated juice. Let this mixture stand for 1 minute, and then stir it. Wait at least 1 minute and then add the boiling water. Stir the mixture for about 5 minutes. Place the fruit at the bottom of each of 6 lunch box containers. Pour on the gelatin mixture. Cover the containers and refrigerate them overnight. This dish is sweet enough to send to school as a dessert.

Yield: About six ½-cup servings

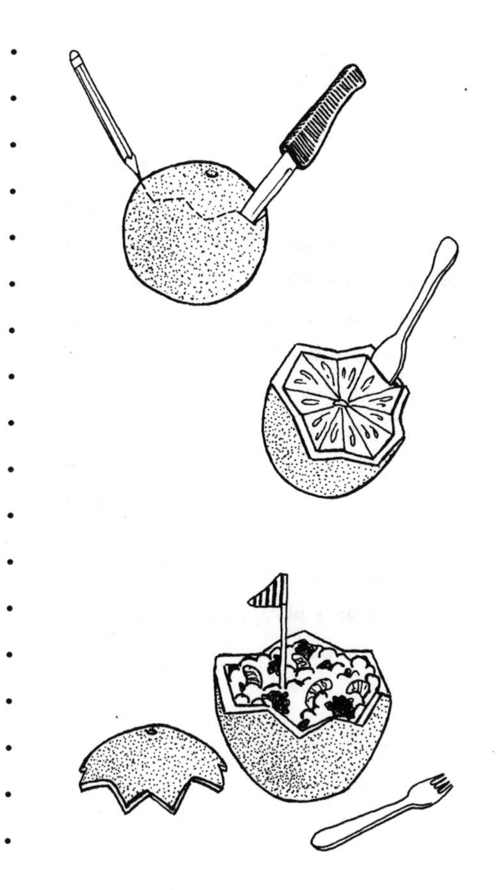

Peach Surprise

Here's a nifty way to liven up your child's lunch. Take a peach and split it open along the seam. Carefully remove the pit, being sure to keep the peach halves intact. Now fill the cavity with a mixture of cottage cheese, raisins, currants, and nuts. Close the peach up again so that it looks like an ordinary peach. Wrap it first in plastic wrap and then in paper towels. If there's room in your child's lunch box, you can put the wrapped peach inside a plastic container to protect it from being squished.

Peachy-Keen Salad

Peaches come into season in late spring and last through the early fall. A ripe peach will be somewhat soft when you squeeze it. This naturally sweet, juicy fruit can be messy to eat by itself, but this salad is easy to eat and delicious.

1/2 cup cottage cheese
2 tablespoons sunflower seeds
1 ripe peach

Put the cottage cheese in a lunch box container. Mix in the sunflower seeds. Cut the peach into bite-size chunks (leave on the skin) and gently toss it into the cottage cheese–sunflower mixture.

Bugs Bunny Salad

• • •

What's up, Doc, is carrots. You can buy them at any time of year and they're packed with vitamins. The nuts in this salad provide additional crunch as well as some protein.

1 carrot
2 tablespoons raisins
2 tablespoons chopped walnuts
Yogurt-Honey Dressing (page 73)

Grate the carrot into a lunch box container. Mix in the raisins and walnuts. Add the dressing and toss.

Veggies Galore

Fresh, uncooked vegetables—you can't serve a more healthful food. In addition to serving vegetables in salads and other dishes, by all means pack raw vegetables in your child's lunch box. Here's how to make the most of vegetables:

• *Wash them well.* Use a vegetable brush to scrub your vegetables clean. This will help get rid of pesticide residues. Do not use soap.

• *Avoid scraping them.* In most cases, the healthiest way to serve vegetables is with the skin on—you lose vitamins when you scrape a carrot or a cucumber. Some kids won't go for the skin, though, and it's better to serve a peeled carrot than no carrot at all.

Dip It!

Are you having trouble getting your kid to eat her vegetables? Here's a fun and healthy way to change her mind. Send her to school with a bag of cut-up vegetables and a little container of dip. It's such an elegant way to eat vegetables! *Note:* Tuna salad (page 39) and egg salad (page 46) both make nice dips; so does flavored yogurt.

Cheese Dip

4 tablespoons cottage cheese
3 tablespoons grated hard cheese
1 teaspoon dried parsley flakes
1/2 teaspoon onion powder

Mix together all the ingredients in a plastic container that you can send to school in your child's lunch box. Refrigerate the dip overnight. *Note:* Parmesan cheese is especially good in this dip.

Yogurt Dip

• • •

¼ cup plain yogurt
¼ teaspoon garlic powder (optional)
¼ cup peeled and diced cucumber
¼ cup minced celery
1 teaspoon green onion

In a lunch box container, mix the yogurt and the garlic powder, if desired. Add the vegetables and blend thoroughly. Refrigerate the dip overnight.

Peanut Butter Dip

• • •

¼ cup peanut butter
¼ cup plain or flavored yogurt
2 tablespoons fruit juice concentrate, thawed

Mix all the ingredients in a lunch box container and refrigerate overnight. This dip goes well with fruit as well as with vegetables.

• ***Cut them into interesting shapes.*** **Although vegetables lose some nutrients when they are peeled and cut, it's worth making them appear more inviting to your child.**

• ***Steam or parboil broccoli and cauliflower.*** **Cut broccoli or cauliflower into florets and steam 2 to 3 minutes, until broccoli turns bright green or cauliflower becomes slightly tender. If you don't have a steamer, drop the vegetable into boiling water and cook 2 to 3 minutes. In either case, after cooking immediately plunge the broccoli or cauliflower into cold water in order to halt the cooking.**

• ***Wrap them in damp paper towels.*** **If you wrap cut vegetables in damp paper towels before wrapping them in plastic or putting them in a lunch box container, they won't dry out as much.**

Apple-Wich

This fruit sandwich is pure fun. Be sure to let your child help make it so she can appreciate its subtler points.

1 apple	*1 tablespoon raisins*
2 tablespoons cottage cheese	*1 tablespoon sunflower seeds*

Cut two wedges from either side of an apple (see illustration). You don't need to worry about the apple turning brown, since the exposed parts will be spread with the filling. In a small bowl, mix together the cottage cheese, raisins, and sunflower seeds. Spread them on the exposed parts of each apple wedge. Now close the apple. At school, your child can open up the apple-wich and eat each half separately.

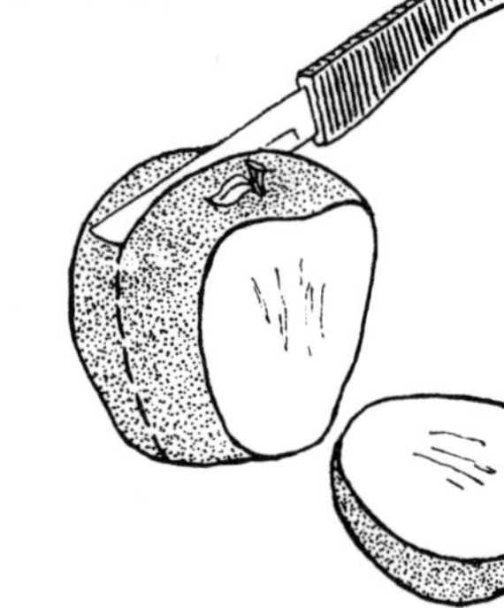

Four-Bean Salad

• • •

This classic salad contains plenty of protein for a meatless meal. It's as easy to make as opening four cans (just about). Since you'll have to open the cans anyway, I've given a recipe for considerably more than you'll need for any one lunch, but this salad fares well for several days in the refrigerator.

1 small (8-ounce) can lima beans
1 small (8-ounce) can kidney beans
1 small (8-ounce) can green beans
1 small (8-ounce) can garbanzo beans (chick-peas)
2 to 3 tablespoons minced onion
2 to 3 tablespoons minced tomato
Tart Dressing (page 75), commercial Italian dressing, Cucumber Dressing (page 74), or dressing of choice

Open the cans and drain the beans. In a medium-size bowl, gently toss all of the ingredients. Four-Bean Salad tastes best if you refrigerate it overnight. Or you could store the cans in the refrigerator so the salad will already be cold when you make it.

Yield: About four 1-cup servings

Baked Potato Surprise

• • •

If your child likes baked potatoes, she'll probably love this baked potato sandwich. Next time you make baked potatoes, pop an extra one in the oven for your child's school lunch.

1 cold baked potato
2 tablespoons grated cheese
2 tablespoons cubed meat (any leftovers will do)
1 tablespoon minced celery
1 to 3 teaspoons sour cream or plain yogurt

Cut the potato in half. Scoop out the potato and set it aside, being careful not to tear the skin. In a small bowl, combine the remaining ingredients, along with a little of the reserved potato. Put the mixture in the potato skin.

Potato Salad Plus

• • •

A side dish of potato salad will give your child the energy she needs to make it through the afternoon as well as vitamins B, C, and G and a number of minerals. Contrary to popular belief, potatoes are not fattening, and neither are the other vegetables in this recipe. If you object to the sour cream, you might try cutting it with plain yogurt.

2 medium-size new potatoes
3 tablespoons sour cream
1 teaspoon red wine vinegar
½ teaspoon onion powder
¼ cup finely chopped green pepper
¼ cup finely chopped red pepper
½ cup broccoli florets, parboiled

Put the potatoes in a saucepan and cover them with water. Bring the water to a boil. Cook the potatoes on a low boil about 45 minutes, or until they are tender right through to the center. Remove the pan to the sink and run cold water on the potatoes for several minutes. Refrigerate them until they're cold. In a medium-size bowl, make a dressing by mixing the sour cream, vinegar, and onion powder. Cut the potatoes into bite-size cubes and add them, the peppers, and the broccoli to the dressing. (To read about parboiling broccoli, see Veggies Galore, page 66.) Toss the salad and refrigerate overnight. This yields enough potato salad for your child's lunch and a side dish on your dinner table.

Yield: Six to eight ½-cup servings

Crunchy Caterpillar

Did anyone say vegetables aren't any fun? Try this version on your child. Cut a carrot into ½-inch chunks and cut ¼-inch slices from a zucchini. Use toothpicks to form a caterpillar's body, using a carrot-zucchini-carrot sequence. Use another toothpick to attach a radish head. Stick on O-shape cereal eyes with cream cheese. Poke small holes in the radish and insert slivers of celery for antennae.

Lettuce Leaf Roll-Ups

Like the Sandwich Roll-Ups on page 51, Lettuce Leaf Roll-Ups are fun to eat. Take a large and firm but pliable lettuce leaf (the outer leaves of Boston lettuce are well suited to the task) and spread it out on a clean surface. Spoon any of the salad recipes given in this chapter into the bottom third of the lettuce leaf. Now roll up the leaf with the mixture inside. Don't try to slice this one—just send it to school as is, tightly wrapped.

Do-It-Yourself Salad

The more decision-making power you give your child, the happier he'll be with the results. So let him decide just what kind of salad he'd like. Put out all the ingredients you have in your fridge and let him make his own salad. In case you're stuck for ideas, here are some ingredients you might use.

Greens
- *Lettuce*
- *Spinach*
- *Cabbage (green or red)*
- *Watercress*

Veggies
- *Sliced carrot, cucumber, mushrooms, radishes*
- *Wedges of tomato*
- *Diced green and red pepper, onion, carrot*
- *Artichoke hearts, asparagus, baby corn*
- *Beans (string, kidney, garbanzo, lima, lentil)*
- *Steamed or parboiled broccoli, cauliflower*
- *Sprouts (beans, alfalfa)*
- *Peas*
- *Cooked, cubed potatoes*

Nuts and Seeds
- *Walnuts, almonds, pecans, peanuts, Brazil nuts, etc.*
- *Sunflower, poppy, sesame seeds*

Meat
- *Cooked, cubed chicken, turkey, ham, roast beef*

Cheese
- *Crumbled farmer's, feta, mozzarella*
- *Grated Muenster, Cheddar, Swiss, etc.*

Dressing

Wash and dry the greens and tear them into bite-size pieces. Put them in a large lunch box container. Put the rest of the ingredients in a smaller lunch box container and toss with the dressing. When your child gets to school, he can pour the contents of the smaller container onto the greens and toss the salad himself. (This way the greens will stay crisp during the morning.)

Salad Dressings

The problem with commercial salad dressings is that they tend to be relatively high in fat (and also sugar and salt). Here are some alternative dressings that please kids' palates. It's worth pointing out, by the way, that the *amount* of dressing you use has a direct bearing on how much fat you introduce to the salad. Even if you use a store-bought dressing, you can keep down the fat content of your child's lunch by using the dressing sparingly. If you're using a creamy store-bought dressing, try thinning it a little with milk.

Yogurt-Honey Dressing

2 tablespoons plain yogurt
1 tablespoon honey

Just mix together.

Citrus Dressing

1 tablespoon plain yogurt
1 tablespoon orange juice concentrate, thawed
1 teaspoon honey

Mix all the ingredients together. This dressing goes especially well with any salad that contains orange or grapefruit sections.

Cucumber Dressing

1 tablespoon plain yogurt
1 tablespoon mayonnaise
1/4 teaspoon minced dried parsley
1/8 teaspoon onion powder
3 tablespoons minced cucumber

Beat together the yogurt, mayonnaise, parsley, and onion powder. Stir in the cucumber. For best results, refrigerate this dressing for a few hours before using it.

Tart Dressing

• • •

1 tablespoon virgin olive oil
1 teaspoon lemon juice
A pinch each dried parsley, basil, dill, and/or thyme

Put all the ingredients in a small lidded jar. Screw on the top and shake well until they're all blended. The lemon in this recipe is less sharp than vinegar, and healthier too.

Banana Dressing

• • •

1/4 ripe banana
1 tablespoon plain yogurt
1 tablespoon cottage cheese
1 teaspoon honey

In a small bowl, mash the banana with the back of a fork. Beat in the yogurt, cottage cheese, and honey. This dressing goes especially well with fruit salads.

Oriental Dressing

• • •

1 tablespoon mayonnaise
1 teaspoon honey
1/2 teaspoon soy sauce

Just mix all the ingredients together. This dressing won't appeal to all children, but those who love Chinese food will probably like it.

7

Hot Meals

On a cold winter's day, there's really no substitute for a good, hot meal. It's not that hot food is any more nutritious than cold—there's just something comforting about a hot meal when it's cold outside.

On the other hand, few of us have the time or energy to prepare an entire hot meal for one school lunch. The recipes on the following pages are very quick and easy. Try making the whole recipe and freezing part of it so that you can serve it over several days. Or serve the bulk of the hot meal to your family at dinner and save a little for your child's school lunch.

I've seen some recipes that suggest that you can cook, for example, a slice of pizza, wrap it in aluminum foil, and expect it to stay warm until lunchtime. My experiments with this technique have been failures. The best way to keep a meal hot is to put it in a thermos. Liquids tend to stay hot longer than solids, so make sure your hot meal is nice and bubbly when you put it in your child's thermos. If the food has dried out during cooking and reheating, add some milk or water when you're reheating it.

Another good thing about hot meals is that they provide a change of pace, not only for your child but for you. Here's a chance to get creative and make something different for your child's school lunch!

Note: Many of these recipes yield several servings. You may want to freeze portions in small plastic containers. If you have a microwave, you could thaw and heat one serving at a time in its own container in the morning. If you don't have a microwave, take the next day's serving out of the freezer and move it to the refrigerator the night before. In the morning, heat it on the stove. To precondition a wide-mouthed thermos, pour boiling water into it, let it sit for a minute, then pour it out before adding the hot food.

Chili and Rice

Some like it hot, some like it mild, but most like it in the lunch box and ready to eat. There's plenty of protein in this dish without the meat—include it if your child likes meat in his chili.

1 cup brown rice
1 tablespoon vegetable oil
1 small onion, chopped
¼ cup chopped green pepper
½ pound ground turkey or hamburger (optional)
1 can (16 ounces) kidney beans
1 can (16 ounces) tomatoes
¼ teaspoon to 1 tablespoon chili powder
Shredded cheese

The night before: Make the rice according to package directions. While it cooks, heat the oil in a medium-size saucepan. Add the onion and green pepper and sauté until the onion softens. Add the meat, if desired, and continue cooking until it is brown and cooked through. Pour off the fat. Add the rest of the ingredients except the cheese, using as much chili powder as you think your child will enjoy. Simmer at least 15 minutes, until chili is thick and hot. Store the cooked rice and chili in separate containers, as described on page 24.

In the morning: Heat the rice and chili separately. Put a layer of rice on the bottom of a preheated wide-mouth thermos. Fill almost to the top with chili. Sprinkle on the cheese and seal the thermos.

Yield: About 3 cups of rice; 5 to 6 cups of chili

Nifty Nachos

• • •

This dish looks like a snack, tastes like junk food, and is actually loaded with protein! Just make sure you shop carefully for tortilla chips that are low in salt and fat.

1/4 cup grated Cheddar cheese
1 small (4-ounce) can refried beans
Tortilla chips

Sprinkle the cheese on the refried beans. Heat at 350° F in the oven or in the microwave on HIGH until the cheese is bubbly. Send the mixture to school in a wide-mouthed thermos. Pack the tortilla chips in a plastic bag.

Hot Diggety Dog

If your child is a hot dog addict, he can get his fix at school as well as at home. Here's all you need to do. Take a clean needle and white thread knotted at the end and sew through the top of the hot dog. Leave about three inches of string hanging loose. Cook the hot dog in simmering water for 5 to 10 minutes. Fill your child's thermos two-thirds to three-quarters full of boiling water. Lower the cooked hot dog into the thermos with the string hanging out. Seal the thermos. Pack a bun spread with mustard, ketchup, pickle relish, and/or whatever else your child likes on his hot dog. At school, he can open the thermos, pull out the hot dog, put it in the bun, remove the thread, and dig in!

Minestrone Soup

This meatless dish contains enough protein to make a substantial lunch. It's easy to make and tastes great.

1 small onion, diced
1 carrot, diced
1 stalk celery, diced
1 zucchini, sliced
2 tablespoons unsaturated oil
1 small potato, diced
1 can (16 ounces) tomatoes
1 can (16 ounces) pinto or kidney beans
1 to 2 cups cooked pasta
Parmesan cheese

The night before: In a medium-size saucepan, sauté the onion, carrot, celery, and zucchini in the oil. Add the potatoes, tomatoes, and beans, and let the soup simmer about 30 minutes to 1 hour, until the potatoes are soft. The soup should have a nice, thick consistency, but if it gets too thick you may need to add a little water. Add the previously cooked pasta and cook for another 5 minutes.

In the morning: Heat the soup and pour it into a preheated wide-mouthed thermos. Sprinkle with the Parmesan cheese. Seal.

Yield: About eight 1-cup servings

Macaroni and Cheese

• • •

Yes, I know . . . packaged macaroni and cheese is a favorite at our house too. But do we really need all that sodium tripolyphosphate, sodium phosphate, and yellow dye numbers 5 and 6? Try this recipe. It tastes great and it's every bit as easy to make as the packaged variety.

2 cups macaroni (or any other kind of pasta your child likes)

1 cup plain yogurt (or sour cream)

2 cups grated Monterey Jack cheese

½ cup bread crumbs

The night before: Cook the macaroni, following the directions on the box. Drain. Preheat the oven to 350° F. Grease a small casserole dish. In a medium-size bowl, mix the yogurt (or sour cream) and 1½ cups cheese. Add the macaroni. Toss until macaroni is well coated. Pour the mixture into the casserole. Sprinkle the remaining ½ cup cheese and the bread crumbs on top. Bake for 30 minutes.

In the morning: Reheat a single serving of macaroni and cheese in the microwave or on the stove. You may want to moisten it with a little milk. Send it to school in a preheated wide-mouthed thermos.

Yield: Six to eight 1-cup servings

(Don't send this treat to school with a child under six, who may not be able to manage the hot water and the string.)

Note: **Other ways to send the hot dog your child craves are to slice it and cook it with baked beans or slice it and add it to a soup (like the Minestrone, following).**

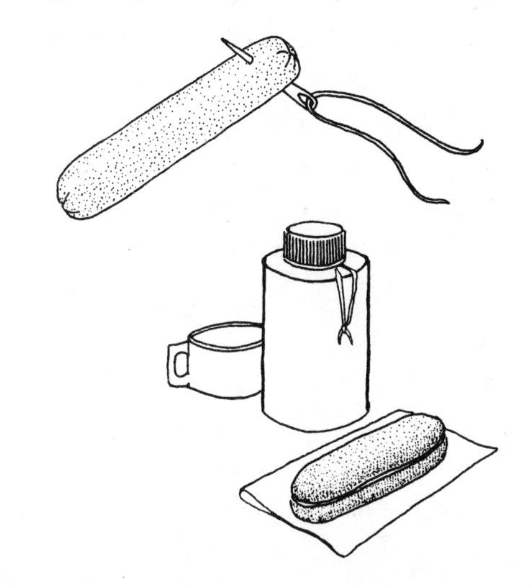

Leftovers

By far the easiest way to send hot food to school with your child is to heat up some leftovers. If your child likes a particular food for dinner, he's likely to enjoy it at lunchtime too. All you have to do is heat up the leftovers and pack them in a wide-mouthed thermos. Be sure to remember to send a fork or spoon along too!

And the next time you send out for Chinese food, don't throw away the leftovers—send them to school with your child.

Ham and Broccoli Soup

If your child likes broccoli, he's sure to like this yummy soup. Ham chunks add flavor and protein. All you need is some bread on the side and a thermos of milk or juice to make this a complete meal.

1 large potato
1 can (15 ounces) chicken broth (undiluted)
1 package (10 ounces) frozen broccoli, thawed
½ cup cooked ham, cut into bite-size chunks
1 cup milk
Croutons

The night before: Peel the potato and cut it into 1-inch chunks. Put them in a medium-size saucepan with the chicken broth and simmer until the potato is cooked through—about 30 minutes. Add the thawed broccoli and heat it through. Put the soup in a blender and whirl for about 1 minute, until the potato is completely broken up and dispersed through the soup. (This makes the soup nice and thick). Return to the pan and add the ham and the milk. Heat through.

In the morning: Heat a serving of soup in the microwave or on top of the stove. Send to school in a preheated wide-mouthed thermos. Pack the croutons separately.

Yield: Five to six 1-cup servings

Taco Time

• • •

Kids love tacos. They're easy to make, fun to eat, taste great, and—if they're made right—can be healthful too. Here's a recipe that uses meat. If you prefer to serve a vegetarian recipe, just heat up some refried beans instead.

1/4 cup diced onion
1 tablespoon vegetable oil
1/2 pound ground turkey or hamburger
1 small (6-ounce) can tomato juice
1/4 to 1 teaspoon chili powder
Preshaped taco shells
Shredded lettuce
Shredded cheese

The night before: Sauté the onion in the oil until it is soft and clear. Add the meat and cook until it is brown and cooked through. Pour off the fat. Add the tomato juice and chili powder and cook another 5 to 10 minutes.

In the morning: Fill each preshaped taco shell with lettuce and cheese. Heat the taco filling and pour into a wide-mouthed thermos. At school, your child can pour the filling into the taco. Or he can add the lettuce and cheese to the taco filling in his thermos and eat it with a fork and pieces of taco shell. You may want to send some mild taco sauce in a separate container.

Yield: 5 or 6 tacos

Here are some leftovers that travel very nicely.

- **Lasagna**
- **Stew**
- **Soup**
- **Mashed potatoes and gravy**
- **Spaghetti and meatballs**
- **Pot roast**
- **Chicken Tetrazzini**
- **Meat loaf**
- **Sloppy Joes (send the bun separately)**
- **Baked beans**

8

Drinks

Most days, your child probably goes to school with either milk or juice in her thermos. But for variety, try some of the alternative drinks listed here. If your kid turns up her nose at fruit, use her drink as an opportunity to get some neglected vitamins into her.

Many of these recipes call for adding an ice cube or two and mixing in a blender. Fresh from the blender, the ice makes the drink frosty and frothy. Some of that lovely texture will be lost as the ice melts during the morning, but the drink will stay nice and cold. To keep the drink as cool as possible, put your child's thermos in the freezer the night before. Make the drink just before your child leaves for school and pack the thermos with other cold foods and an ice pack.

Or you can eliminate the ice and put the blended drink in a thermos in the freezer. The next morning pack the thermos in your child's lunch box. The drink will thaw during the morning.

In any case, tell your child to give her sealed thermos a good shake before she opens it.

St. Patrick's Day Surprise

Schoolyard legend has it that you have to wear green on St. Patrick's Day. Why not add something green to your child's lunch? To be fair, you should give her some kind of advance warning, if only by putting a shamrock sticker on the top of the thermos.

1 cup Banana Drink (at right)
A few drops green food color

Just mix in the food color until the drink turns a lovely green!

Banana Drink

If your kid prefers chocolate milk to plain milk, offer this drink as an alternative. The banana makes the milk taste sweet and thick without that bad, bad chocolate.

3/4 cup milk
1/2 ripe banana
1/2 teaspoon vanilla
A pinch of cinnamon
1 ice cube

Put all the ingredients in the blender and mix until the drink is nice and smooth. Pour immediately into a prefrozen thermos.

Daiquiri Delight

This drink is slightly exotic and oh-so-sophisticated.

1/3 cup apple juice
1/3 cup orange juice
1/4 small banana
1 to 2 ice cubes

Put everything in the blender and blend for a few seconds until all the ingredients are smooth. Pour the drink into a prechilled thermos.

Fruity Milk Drink

This is a good choice for the kid on the go who can barely stand to eat his lunch before hitting the recess yard. The frozen juice is the equivalent of a cup of juice. If your child can sit still long enough to drink this and eat a sandwich, he'll be in pretty good shape for the rest of the afternoon.

¾ cup milk
¼ cup frozen juice concentrate (apple, pear, grape, etc.)

Just blend the ingredients in a blender. Then pack in a prechilled thermos.

Hot Spiced Apple Juice

Here's a nice hot drink for a cold winter's day.

1 cup apple juice
¼ teaspoon cinnamon
⅛ teaspoon nutmeg

Heat all the ingredients to boiling and pour them in a preheated thermos. (To preheat, fill the thermos with boiling water and then pour it out just before adding hot apple juice.)

For an alternative method, heat the apple juice, pour it in your child's thermos, and drop a cinnamon stick in before sealing the thermos.

Juice Cubes

Here's a way to make sure your child's juice stays cold without becoming diluted. Pour juice into ice cube trays and freeze them. Then just pop some juice cubes in your child's thermos when you pack her juice. You may want to use minicube trays or half-filled conventional trays to make sure the cubes fit through the mouth of the thermos.

Choosing Milk and Juices

Here's how to make sure you buy the best drink for your child.

• *Use lowfat milk.* After age two, children should be given skim or 2 percent milk instead of whole milk, which has too much fat and cholesterol.

• *Use real fruit juice.* When you shop for juices, make sure to look for 100 percent real fruit juice. There are many products masquerading as juice that actually contain only a small percentage of fruit juice. If you see the word *drink* or *ade* you'll know you're not buying 100 percent juice.

Melon Mix

Melons are abundant in the summertime; this is a good drink to think of for summer camp days. Look for a brand of grape juice that hasn't been sweetened—either artificially or naturally. Grapes are naturally sweet.

1/2 cup mixed chunks of melon (without the seeds)—cantaloupe, honeydew, casaba, and/or watermelon
1/2 cup grape juice
1 ice cube

Put all the ingredients in the blender and mix thoroughly. Pour immediately into a prechilled thermos.

Yogurt Shake

• • •

Here's a drink that's as rich and smooth as a milkshake but much healthier.

1/2 cup plain or flavored yogurt
1/2 cup frozen berries (strawberries, raspberries, or blueberries), frozen pineapple, or frozen peaches
1/4 teaspoon vanilla
Milk (optional)
Honey to taste

Put the yogurt, fruit, and vanilla in a blender and mix until the drink is smooth. The juice from the fruit should dilute the yogurt and make it drinkable. If not, add a little milk. Add a teaspoon of honey, and taste. Add more as needed (it will depend on how sweet the fruit is).

• *Read the labels.* Cranberry juice provides plenty of vitamin C and is a nice alternative to orange juice. Unfortunately, cranberries are so sour that manufacturers add sugar to create the ubiquitous cranberry juice "cocktail." A few companies market mixed fruit drinks that use apple, pear, or other juices to naturally sweeten the cranberries.

• *Check out the exotic fruit nectars at your grocery store and find out whether your child will drink them.* Watch out, though, for commercial sweetening in these drinks too.

• *Try white grape juice.* Purple grape juice can stain children's teeth as well as their clothing. White grape juice is a better choice.

9

Quick Breads and Muffins

I love to make quick breads and muffins with my daughter. The recipes offered here are much faster and easier to prepare than yeast breads. It takes just a few minutes to mix the batter, pour it into pans, and pop them in the oven. Then all you have to do is wait for the delicious aroma of baking to fill your home!

Baking is a terrific way to keep kids busy on a rainy afternoon or snowy day. Using fruit and vegetables in your breads and muffins is also a nice way to introduce your child to some new tastes. The child who usually won't touch zucchini, for example, may relish a steaming slice of zucchini bread.

Most of these recipes call for some sugar or other sweetener. Depending on your personal standards, you may decide to serve the sweeter muffins and breads only as desserts. Or you may feel that an occasional sandwich of tuna fish salad on carrot bread is worth the price of a little extra sugar in your child's diet. I have kept the sugar content in these recipes down to what I consider a reasonable minimum, but you can always reduce or increase the sugar content further to suit your family's taste.

All of the recipes include some fat too, so take this into account as you plan the rest of your child's meal.

Baking Hints

Here's how to make sure your bread and muffins come out just right.

• ***Preheat the oven.*** **Turn the oven on at least 10 to 15 minutes before you start mixing the ingredients.**

• ***Grease the pan.*** **Use margarine or a polyunsaturated vegetable oil such as sunflower or safflower oil.**

• ***Use muffin tin liners.*** **These little paper liners make clean-up a breeze. You can send the muffins to school right in the liners. (If you want to make clean-up even easier, use disposable aluminum loaf or muffin pans.)**

Whole-Wheat–Apple Bread

Nutritious whole-wheat flour combines with flavorful, vitamin-packed apples in this tasty recipe. I like to leave the skins on the apples, but you may prefer to peel them.

1/2 cup margarine
1/2 to 1 cup sugar
2 eggs
2 tablespoons buttermilk
1 teaspoon vanilla
1 cup all-purpose flour
3/4 cup whole-wheat flour
1 teaspoon baking soda
1 teaspoon ground cinnamon
1/2 teaspoon salt
2 cups chopped apples

In a large bowl, mash the margarine with the back of a fork. Then stir in the sugar, eggs, buttermilk, and vanilla. In a medium-size bowl, combine the flours, baking soda, cinnamon, and salt. Add the flour mixture to the margarine mixture and stir. Mix in the apples. Pour the batter into a greased loaf pan. Bake at 350° F for about 70 minutes.

Fun-to-Make Carrot Bread

There's only 1/4 cup of honey in this recipe—the sweetness comes from the banana and the raisins. Your child will get a little fruit, a little vegetable, a little whole grain, and even some yogurt when he eats this yummy bread. Try it with ham and cheese or tuna fish!

1/4 cup margarine
1/4 cup honey
1 egg
1 ripe banana
1/3 cup plain yogurt or buttermilk
1 teaspoon vanilla
1 cup all-purpose flour
1 cup whole-wheat flour
1 teaspoon baking soda
1 teaspoon baking powder
1/4 teaspoon salt
1/2 teaspoon ground nutmeg
1 cup grated carrots
1/2 cup raisins

In a large bowl, mash the margarine with the back of a fork. Beat in the honey and the egg. Beat in the banana, mashing it with the back of the fork. Stir in the yogurt or buttermilk and the vanilla. In a medium-size bowl, combine the flours, baking soda, baking powder, salt, and nutmeg. Pour the flour mixture into the large bowl and combine it with the egg-banana mixture. Add the carrots and raisins. Now comes the fun part. It's hard to mix these ingredients successfully with a spoon. So let your child knead them together with his (clean!) hands. Pour the batter into a greased loaf pan. Bake at 350° F for about 1 hour.

- ***Don't overmix.*** **Just fold the ingredients together gently until the flour is moistened. Don't worry about lumps.**
- ***Use the middle rack of your oven.*** **This will ensure that the heat circulates evenly around the bread or muffins.**
- ***Don't taste the batter!*** **I know it's hard to resist, but any batter containing raw eggs poses a risk of salmonella poisoning.**

Blueberry Muffins

Fresh blueberries are at their peak in summer, but you can buy frozen blueberries all year round and they're almost as good. If you're using frozen blueberries, don't thaw them out—they'll hold up better if you leave them frozen when you mix up the recipe.

2 eggs
1/4 cup melted margarine
1/3 to 2/3 cup sugar
3/4 cup milk
1 teaspoon vanilla
1 3/4 cups all-purpose flour
2 teaspoons baking powder
3/4 teaspoon salt
1 cup fresh or frozen blueberries

In a small bowl, beat the eggs. Stir in the melted margarine, sugar, milk, and vanilla. In a large bowl, combine the flour, baking powder, and salt. Spoon the egg mixture into the flour mixture and mix until all the ingredients are moist. Gently fold in the blueberries. Spoon the batter into 12 greased or lined muffin tins. Bake at 400° F for about 20 minutes.

Banana–Wheat Germ Bread

This classic is easy to make and sure to please. The riper the bananas, the more flavorful the bread will be.

- *1/3 cup margarine*
- *1/4 to 3/4 cup golden brown sugar, packed*
- *2 eggs*
- *2 ripe bananas*
- *1 teaspoon vanilla*
- *1/2 cup chopped nuts*
- *1 1/2 cups all-purpose flour*
- *1/4 cup wheat germ*
- *2 teaspoons baking powder*
- *1/4 teaspoon baking soda*
- *1/2 teaspoon salt*
- *1/2 teaspoon ground cinnamon*

In a large bowl, mash the margarine with the back of a fork. Beat in the sugar and eggs. Add the bananas and beat them in, mashing them with the back of the fork. Stir in the vanilla and then the nuts. In a medium-size bowl, mix the flour, wheat germ, baking powder, baking soda, salt, and cinnamon. Pour the flour mixture into the large bowl and blend all the ingredients together. Pour the batter into a greased loaf pan. Bake at 350° F for about 55 minutes.

How to Convert to Whole-Wheat Flour

Whole-wheat flour, which contains the bran and the germ of wheat, is more nutritious than ordinary white flour. Most children who have been raised on white flour find whole wheat alone a bit too "strange." Try adding just a little whole wheat to recipes that call for flour and build up your child's acceptance level. Here's how to convert to whole wheat.

All-Purpose White Flour	=	Whole-Wheat Flour
1/4 cup		3 tablespoons
1/2 cup		6 tablespoons
1 cup		3/4 cup
2 cups		1 1/2 cups

Zucchini Bread

Sometime around the end of summer, if you know anyone who gardens, you're bound to have more zucchinis on your hands than you know what to do with. Even if your child is a good vegetable eater, he'll probably rebel about the third time you serve steamed zucchini at supper. Maybe this bread will change his tune. Bake a couple of these loaves and freeze one until later in the year!

1/3 cup margarine
1/2 to 1 cup sugar
2 eggs
1/3 cup water
1 teaspoon vanilla
1 1/2 cups grated zucchini
1/3 cup chopped walnuts
1/3 cup raisins
3/4 cup all-purpose flour
3/4 cup whole-wheat flour
1 teaspoon baking soda
1 teaspoon baking powder
3/4 teaspoon salt
1/2 teaspoon ground cloves
1/4 teaspoon ground cinnamon
1/4 teaspoon ground nutmeg

In a large bowl, mash the margarine with the back of a fork. Mix in the sugar. Add the eggs, water, and vanilla, and stir until the batter is smooth. Stir in the zucchini, walnuts, and raisins. In a medium-size bowl, combine the flours, baking soda, baking powder, salt, cloves, cinnamon, and nutmeg. Add the flour mixture to the zucchini mixture and fold the two mixtures together gently. Pour the batter into a greased loaf pan. Bake for about 1 hour at 350° F.

Naturally Sweet Pineapple Muffins

• • •

You'll be amazed at how sweet these muffins taste with just pineapple juice as a sweetener.

1/2 cup margarine
3 eggs
1 large (20-ounce) can crushed pineapple (in natural juice)
2 1/2 cups all-purpose flour
2 teaspoons baking powder
1 teaspoon baking soda

In a large bowl, mash the margarine with the back of a fork. Beat in the eggs. Thoroughly drain the crushed pineapple, being careful to reserve the drained juice. Add 1 cup of pineapple juice to the margarine-egg mixture. In a medium-size bowl, combine the flour, baking powder, and baking soda. Pour the flour mixture into the egg mixture. Fold in the drained pineapple. Pour this batter into 12 greased or lined muffin tins. Bake at 350° F for about 25 minutes.

Freeze It!

You don't have to make up a fresh batch of muffins or bread every few days. Make plenty when you do bake and freeze some. Follow these guidelines:

- ***Let them cool before freezing.*** **Almost every muffin and bread recipe advises readers to let breads and muffins cool before eating, but who can sit around waiting for something delicious to cool? Breads and muffins taste best when they're steamy from the oven. When you're freezing, however, do let them cool completely at room temperature before wrapping them.**

Cranberry-Orange Bread

I always make this bread at Thanksgiving and somehow I keep on making it through the new year. It tastes great with turkey and the other roasts we tend to make around the holidays. It's also very low in fat. Cranberries freeze well, so stick a bag in your freezer and make more cranberry-orange bread in the spring!

2 cups all-purpose flour
1/2 to 1 cup sugar
1 1/2 teaspoons baking powder
1/2 teaspoon baking soda
1/2 teaspoon salt
2 tablespoons margarine
1 egg
3/4 cup orange juice
1 1/2 tablespoons grated orange rind
1 cup chopped cranberries
1/2 cup chopped walnuts, pecans, or other nuts

In a large bowl, mix the flour, sugar, baking powder, baking soda, and salt. Cut in the margarine and blend until it is evenly distributed. In a small bowl, beat the egg. Beat in the orange juice and orange rind. Pour the orange juice mixture into the large bowl and mix it with the flour mixture. Stir in the cranberries and the nuts. Pour the batter into a greased loaf pan. Bake at 350°F for about 1 hour.

Raisin Bran Muffins

• • •

If your child likes raisin bran at breakfast, he'll love raisin bran muffins at lunchtime. These muffins are easy to make and are especially fragrant and chewy.

2½ cups raisin bran
1 cup milk
⅓ cup honey
1 egg
3 tablespoons vegetable oil
1¼ cups all-purpose flour
1 tablespoon baking powder
¼ teaspoon salt

Put the raisin bran in a medium-size bowl and pour on the milk. Let this mixture sit for a few minutes while you prepare the other ingredients. In a small bowl, mix the honey, egg, and oil. In a large bowl, mix the flour, baking powder, and salt. Add the contents of the small- and medium-size bowls to the large bowl, and mix until all the ingredients are blended. Pour the batter into 12 greased or lined muffin tins. Bake at 400° F for 15 to 20 minutes.

• *Wrap them.* Once they've cooled, wrap your bread or muffins in a layer of plastic wrap and then a double layer of aluminum foil. You may want to wrap muffins individually so you can take them out of the freezer as needed. You can slice bread and wrap the slices individually too.

• *Use them within six weeks of baking.* If you take the bread or muffins out of the freezer and put them in the refrigerator the night before, they will be thawed by the time your child leaves for school. In warm weather, put frozen bread or muffins in your child's lunch box. It should thaw by the time your child sits down to eat.

Are They Done Yet?

No two stoves are exactly alike, so no cookbook can tell you precisely how long something will take to cook in your oven. Rather than relying exclusively on the cooking times given here, use your own judgment to determine whether bread or muffins are ready. The tops of the bread or muffins should be golden brown and they should pull away slightly from the sides of the pan. When you insert a toothpick in a muffin or a loaf of bread, it should come out clean. If you're testing bread, make sure your toothpick goes deep into the center of the bread.

Peanut Butter Bread

If your child is a true peanut butter–aholic, she'll probably want peanut butter and jelly on peanut butter bread! Try to get her to experiment a little—with a cream cheese/raisin spread or cottage cheese and apple. You can use crunchy or smooth peanut butter in this recipe.

1 egg
1/2 cup peanut butter
1/4 cup honey
3/4 cup milk
2 cups all-purpose flour
2 teaspoons baking powder
1/2 teaspoon baking soda
1/2 teaspoon salt

In a large bowl, beat the egg. Then mix in the peanut butter, honey, and milk. In a medium-size bowl, combine the flour, baking powder, baking soda, and salt. Then add the flour mixture to the peanut butter mixture. Mix until all the dry ingredients have been moistened. When the dough is smooth and elastic, spoon it into a greased loaf pan. Bake at 350° F for about 45 minutes.

Ham 'n' Corn Muffins

This combination of ham, corn, and cornmeal offers high-quality protein your child can sink his teeth into. There's almost no sugar in these muffins—they're practically a main course in themselves.

- *2 eggs*
- *1/2 cup melted margarine*
- *1 1/2 cups buttermilk*
- *3/4 cup frozen corn kernels, thawed*
- *1/2 cup shredded ham*
- *1 cup cornmeal*
- *1 cup all-purpose flour*
- *1 1/2 tablespoons sugar*
- *2 teaspoons baking powder*
- *1 teaspoon baking soda*
- *1/2 teaspoon salt*

In a large bowl, beat the eggs. Add the melted butter and buttermilk and stir. Stir in the corn and the ham. In a medium-size bowl, combine the cornmeal, flour, sugar, baking powder, baking soda, and salt. Pour the cornmeal mixture into the ham-and-corn mixture, and gently stir until all the dry ingredients are mixed in. Pour into 12 greased or lined muffin tins. Bake at 400° F for 25 minutes.

Banana-Coconut Muffins

Just wait until your family smells these muffins cooking. You'll be lucky to have enough left over to send in your child's lunch box the next day!

1 egg
1/2 cup melted margarine
1/2 cup sugar
1/2 cup buttermilk
3/4 teaspoon vanilla
1 ripe banana
1 cup unsweetened (or sweetened) shredded coconut
1 1/2 cups all-purpose flour
1 teaspoon baking soda
1 1/2 teaspoons baking powder
1/4 teaspoon salt
1/2 teaspoon ground cinnamon

In a large bowl, beat the egg. Stir in the melted margarine, the sugar, buttermilk, and vanilla. Add the banana, mashing and mixing it with the back of a fork. Mix in the coconut. In a medium-size bowl, mix the flour, baking soda, baking powder, salt, and cinnamon. Add the flour mixture to the mixture in the large bowl and gently fold the two together. Pour the batter into 12 greased or lined muffin tins. Bake at 375° F for 25 minutes.

10 Something Extra

My informal survey of schoolchildren found that most like to bring at least three items in their lunch boxes: a sandwich or other main course, "something extra," and either a sweet (like cookies) or a piece of fruit. This chapter is about the something extra, which might be a bag of popcorn, some celery with a cheese spread, or slices of green bell pepper.

A few of the children I met seemed to have lunches composed entirely of extras. One child was eating strips of steak, cubes of pineapple, carrot sticks, and a roll—a perfectly healthy way to eat. Most children like to snack, and filling their lunch boxes with extras is a good way of making school lunches inviting.

Popcorn and . . .

Popcorn is the snack food with the dark, unmentionable secret: It's good for you. The basic food—popped corn—is filling and nutritious. It's another story, though, when you load it up with butter and salt. Pop up some corn (preferably in a hot-air popper) and send some to school as is in your child's lunch. Or try one of these recipes.

Note: Send ½ to 1 cup of any of these recipes in a plastic container with a lid or a sandwich bag. Store the rest in a lidded jar. The first three recipes will keep in your refrigerator for at least a week. You can store the last recipe in the cupboard for several weeks.

Cheesy Popcorn

4 cups popped popcorn
1½ tablespoons margarine
¼ cup grated Parmesan cheese

Put the popped popcorn in a large bowl. Melt the margarine and stir in the Parmesan cheese. Pour the cheese mixture over the popcorn and toss.

Nacho Popcorn

Use the same recipe as for Cheesy Popcorn but add ¼ to 1 teaspoon chili powder to the margarine-cheese mixture.

Popcorn, Peanut Butter, and Jelly

4 cups popped popcorn
1 tablespoon margarine
2 teaspoons peanut butter
1 teaspoon jelly
½ cup peanuts

While the popcorn is popping, melt the margarine. Stir in the peanut butter and jelly. While all the ingredients are still warm, toss the peanuts and the peanut butter and jelly mixture into the popcorn.

Protein Pinwheel

Here's a fun way to get some protein into your kid. Take a slice of lunch meat and a slice of cheese and roll them up like a jelly roll. Now cut ½-inch slices from the roll, securing each pinwheel with a toothpick.

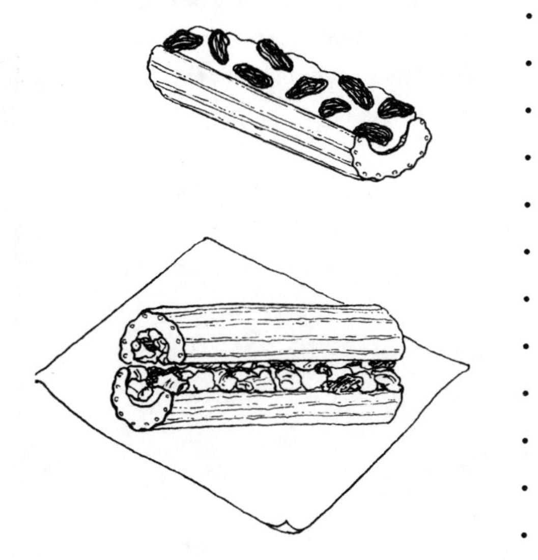

Popcorn Blend

2 cups popped popcorn
1 cup pretzel sticks
½ cup nuts

In a large bowl, toss all the ingredients.

Ants on a Log

For young chefs, especially preschoolers, Ants on a Log is a culinary achievement. Make sure to let your youngster help make this picnic-inspired treat.

Celery
Cream cheese or peanut butter
Raisins

Wash the celery well and trim any strings. Cut it into manageable (about 3-inch) sections. Spread the celery with cream cheese or peanut butter and then decorate with raisin "ants." (See Celery and . . . , on the opposite page, for packing tips.)

Peanut Butter Balls

These crunchy treats are yummy enough to serve as a dessert, but they're healthful enough to eat as a snack.

1/4 cup granola
1/4 cup wheat germ
2 tablespoons brown sugar, packed
1/4 cup dry skim milk powder
1/4 cup sesame seeds
1/4 cup raisins
3/4 cup peanut butter
1/2 cup unsweetened shredded coconut

In a medium-size bowl, mix the granola, wheat germ, brown sugar, skim milk powder, and sesame seeds. Toss in the raisins. Now add the peanut butter a little at a time till it forms a smooth, pliable mixture. Form into balls, using about 1 teaspoon of the mixture per ball. Roll the peanut butter balls in the coconut. Store in the refrigerator overnight.

Yield: 2 to 3 dozen balls

Celery and . . .

It seems as if nature planned celery so that it could be stuffed. You've probably already offered your child peanut butter and celery, but have you thought about other combinations? Any of the Cream Cheese and . . . combinations (see page 38) will work nicely with celery, as will the egg salad mixture (page 46), the tuna fish mixture (page 39) and the dips (page 66). Don't fill the celery to overflowing, or it will be hard to eat. Pack two stuffed celery pieces with the fillings facing each other, so they don't get smeared on the wrapping.

Good and Bad Convenience Foods

Kids love packaged convenience foods. Parents generally hate them because they are (a) expensive and (b) frequently unhealthful. If, however, you're willing to pay for some extra convenience and want to please your child, you can serve any of these convenience foods without losing your peace of mind.

- **Unsweetened applesauce in 4-ounce containers**
- **"String cheese" (sticks of mozzarella)**
- **Pregrated cheese (Cheddar, Swiss, etc.)**
- **Fruit juice–sweetened cookies**
- **Miniature boxes of raisins**
- **Plain, unroasted nuts**

Oven-Fried Chicken

A piece of chicken is the perfect way to send a helping of protein to school in your child's lunch box. When you cook chicken with the skin on, you'll find that there's more than enough fat on the chicken itself—there's no reason to fry it in oil and make it greasy. Use this oven-frying method so that you don't have to use any additional fat.

1/2 cup all-purpose flour
1/4 teaspoon paprika
1/4 teaspoon salt
1/4 teaspoon pepper
1/4 teaspoon garlic powder
1 teaspoon dried parsley
4 chicken legs and 4 chicken thighs
1/2 cup milk

Optional:
1/2 cup milk
1 egg
1/2 cup of any combination of the following: bread crumbs, crushed crackers, cornflake crumbs, graham cracker crumbs, cornmeal, wheat germ, Parmesan cheese, sesame seeds, poppy seeds, crushed nuts

Preheat oven to 400° F. Put the flour, paprika, salt, pepper, garlic powder, and parsley in a sturdy, clean paper bag, and shake it to mix all the ingredients. Wash and dry the chicken pieces and dunk them in the milk. Then shake them in the flour mixture.

If you want to make the chicken extra crunchy: Beat the additional ½ cup milk with the egg. Make your own combination of bread crumbs, crushed crackers, and so on. Dunk the chicken pieces in the milk-egg mixture and then roll them in the crumbs.

Put the coated or uncoated chicken pieces on an oven-proof cooking dish with a rack and bake for about 45 minutes. They're done when they're lightly browned and slightly plumped up and when the juice runs clear when you poke them with a fork. Refrigerate overnight. Send a piece of chicken to school in a well-insulated, cool lunch box. You can freeze individual pieces of chicken and pack the frozen pieces in your child's lunch.

Yield: 8 pieces of chicken

- **Miniature cans of fruit or fruit salad, unsweetened, in pull-top cans**
- **Cans and boxes of unsweetened fruit juice**
- **Salt-free vegetable juice**
- **Low-salt pretzels**

Here are some convenience foods to avoid:

- **Fruit-shaped and -flavored candies masquerading as fruit**
- **Sugar-laced granola bars**
- **Cheese spread**
- **Packaged cupcakes, fruit pies, toaster tarts, and so on**
- **Soda, including diet soda and "natural" sodas**
- **Chocolate- or yogurt-covered nuts or raisins (except as dessert)**
- **Roasted, salted nuts**
- **Drinks and ades that contain less than 100 percent real fruit juice**

Easter Surprises

At Easter, the decorating begins with eggs, but it needn't stop there. Here's a basketful of ideas:

• *Easter eggs.* Hard-boiled eggs don't travel especially well, so if you want to send a decorated egg, wrap it in several layers of paper towels and then some plastic wrap. Even more important, make sure your child's lunch box is well cooled and insulated.

• *Plastic eggs.* The Easter display at your local variety store probably offers packs of plastic snap-apart Easter eggs. Put a note in a plastic egg and pack it in your child's lunch. Or fill an egg with GORP, another snack, or maybe a small Easter candy.

Chicken Chunks

These Chicken Chunks taste every bit as good as the kind You Know McWho makes.

1 boneless chicken breast
2 tablespoons all-purpose flour
Pinch of salt
Pinch of pepper
2 tablespoons milk
1 egg (optional)
1/2 cup bread crumbs
Ketchup, barbecue sauce, or sweet-and-sour sauce

Wash the chicken breast and dry it, then cut it into bite-size chunks. In a shallow bowl, mix the flour, salt, and pepper. Dredge the chicken in the flour mixture. Place the milk and egg, if desired, in a small bowl. Dunk the chicken nuggets in the milk (or milk-egg mixture) and then roll them in the bread crumbs. At this point, you can freeze the nuggets.

To prepare: Put as many nuggets as your child wants for lunch on a cookie sheet. Bake at 425° F for 10 to 15 minutes. (Cut into one to make sure it is cooked through.) Wrap the cooled nuggets in foil and send them to school in a cool, insulated lunch box. Send along a small container of ketchup, barbecue sauce, or sweet-and-sour sauce.

Yield: About four 6-nugget servings

Apple Crunchies

• • •

There are plenty of different textures in this snack: hard, juicy apples, sticky peanut butter, and light, airy rice cereal. Try it!

3 tablespoons peanut butter *1 apple*
3 tablespoons rice cereal

In a small bowl, mix the peanut butter and the rice cereal. Cut the apple into large cubes and add them to the peanut butter–cereal mixture. Toss until the cubes are covered. Send to school in a plastic container.

• *Easter grass.* Use colorful Easter grass when you pack your child's lunch. You might line her lunch box with grass. Or fill a small plastic container with grass and place red and green grapes in this "nest."

• *Easter basket.* On the day before school lets out for Easter break, you might let your child bring her lunch to school in last year's Easter basket.

And Don't Forget . . .

There are probably lots of foods your child likes to snack on that could easily fit into her lunch box. Here are some possibilities:

- **Bread sticks**
- **Low-fat, low-salt crackers**
- **Low-salt pretzels**
- **Trail mix**
- **Nuts**
- **Seeds**
- **Raisins**
- **Cereal**
- **Dried fruit**

GORP

I had heard of GORP for years but it was only last summer, when my daughter was in camp, that I finally found out that the initials stand for "Good Old Raisins and Peanuts." GORP makes a terrific snack food any time of day. You might want to send some extra GORP along to school with your child in case he gets hungry on the school bus coming home. If you add coconut and carob chips, it becomes a dessert. GORP is also a good way to get rid of the not-quite-a-bowlful of cereal that tends to linger uneaten on the kitchen shelf.

1 cup assorted breakfast cereals
1/4 cup sesame seeds
1/2 cup peanuts
1/2 cup raisins
1/2 cup coconut (optional)
1/2 cup carob chips (optional)

In a large bowl, combine all the ingredients. Pour the contents into a big lidded jar and store up to two months, doling out portions of approximately 1/2 cup for your child's lunch. Send GORP to school in a lidded plastic container or a sandwich bag.

To compete with the individually wrapped, store-bought snacks, try to pack these snacks creatively. You could, for instance, take a large square of origami paper, put some raisins in the center, gather up the paper, and tie it with a piece of yarn or ribbon. Or put some pretzels or GORP in an envelope, seal it, and address the envelope to your child, care of her lunch box, the cafeteria, her school, your town. None of these snacks is perishable, so you can pack extra for your child's on-the-way-home-from-school treat.

11

Desserts

Among my friends who have children, there is considerable disagreement on the issue of desserts. Some are rigidly anti-sweets and refuse to allow their children any cookies or candy, except on rare occasions, such as birthdays. Others have a completely laissez-faire attitude and allow their children unlimited access to the family cookie jar. Most believe (as I do) in allowing sweets in moderation.

There's no "right" amount of sweets, because every child is different. If your child has a weight problem or is prone to tooth decay, you may feel you need to restrict sweets. If your child is extremely active and/or aggressive, you may want to consult his pediatrician about whether sugar could play a role in his behavior.

When I was compiling recipes for this book, I tracked down quite a few sugar-free desserts and tried them out on my family one week. "This would taste pretty good if you added some sugar," my husband said. My daughter's response was a less measured "Yuck!" The troops grew increasingly restless, and by Friday both my daughter and my husband were threatening to move to Granny's house until I finished my research.

Here are a range of recipes, from the best sugar-free or low-sugar recipes I could find, to moderately sweet desserts, to no-holds-barred indulgences. You can always increase or decrease the sugar content when you make the recipes yourself.

Dessert Crêpes

Here's a fancy dessert that is surprisingly low in sugar.

2 eggs
1 1/4 cups milk
3/4 cup whole-wheat flour
1/2 teaspoon salt
Fruit-sweetened jelly
Powdered sugar and/or cinnamon

In a medium-size bowl, beat the eggs. Beat in the milk and add the flour and salt. Let the crêpe batter stand about 5 minutes. Then cook the crêpes quickly in a lightly greased frying pan or griddle, over high heat. Spread each crêpe with fruit-sweetened jelly and roll it up. Sprinkle on some powdered sugar and/or cinnamon. Wrap each crêpe in waxed paper and plastic wrap.

Yield: About 12 crêpes

Frosty Peach Dessert

Here's another good choice if you're avoiding sugar.

1 ripe peach
1/3 cup plain or vanilla yogurt
1/4 teaspoon ground cinnamon

Remove the skin and pit from the peach. Put all the ingredients in the blender and blend until smoothly mixed. Pour the frothy results into a thermos and freeze overnight. Pack this treat in your child's lunch box the next morning.

Whole-Wheat–Oatmeal Cookies

These oatmeal cookies are packed with goodness—oats, whole-wheat flour and wheat germ, raisins and nuts. And they're chewy and good too.

1/4 cup margarine
1/2 cup brown sugar, packed
1 egg
1/2 teaspoon vanilla
1/4 cup whole-wheat flour
1/2 cup wheat germ
3/4 cup rolled oats
1/2 teaspoon baking powder
A pinch of salt
1/2 cup raisins
1/4 cup chopped walnuts, pecans, or other nuts

In a large bowl, mash the margarine with the back of a fork. Stir in the brown sugar, egg, and vanilla. In a medium-size bowl, mix the flour, wheat germ, oats, baking powder, and salt. Pour the flour mixture into the margarine mixture and stir until blended. Fold in the raisins and nuts. Drop teaspoonfuls onto a greased cookie sheet and bake at 375° F for about 10 minutes.

Yield: 2 to 3 dozen

Wigglies

These wiggly blocks of hardened gelatin taste like candy, but they're made with fruit juice and unflavored gelatin.

4 cups fruit juice | *4 envelopes unflavored gelatin*

Pour 1 cup fruit juice in a large bowl and sprinkle on the gelatin. Let stand for at least 1 minute. Meanwhile, heat the remaining 3 cups of juice to boiling. Add the hot juice to the mixture in the bowl and stir until all the gelatin has dissolved. Pour the mixture into a 9×13-inch pan. Refrigerate until the gelatin has completely cooled. Now cut it into blocks or use your cookie cutters to make interesting shapes. Store the cubes in plastic bags.

Yield: About 50 wigglies, depending on the size

Halloween Cupcakes

Your little ghost or goblin will enjoy this yummy treat at Halloween. And you'll appreciate the fact that he's getting a goodie that's somewhat more nourishing than candy. You may want to whip up a big batch of these and hand them out to your neighborhood ghouls on trick-or-treat night.

1/2 cup margarine
2 eggs
1 cup brown sugar, packed
3/4 cup canned pumpkin
1 3/4 cups all-purpose flour
1 teaspoon baking soda
1/2 teaspoon salt
1/2 teaspoon ground cinnamon
1/2 teaspoon ground nutmeg
1/2 teaspoon ground cloves
Vanilla frosting or 4 ounces of cream cheese
Red and yellow food coloring
Candy corns and/or raisins

In a large bowl, mash the margarine with the back of a fork. Beat in the eggs, brown sugar, and pumpkin. In a medium-size bowl, mix the flour, baking soda, salt, and spices. Pour the flour mixture into the large bowl and mix to combine ingredients. Pour the batter into 12 to 18 paper-lined muffin tins and bake at 350° F for about 20 minutes, until a toothpick comes out clean.

When the cupcakes have cooled, mix a few drops of red and yellow food coloring into a bowl of homemade or packaged vanilla frosting or cream cheese until you have a nice orange frosting. Frost the cupcakes and then decorate them with the candy corns and/or raisins. Make cheery or scary Jack-o'-lantern faces in the frosting!

Yield: 12 to 18 cupcakes

Cone Cakes

Your child will get a kick out of this different way to make cupcakes. This is a great treat to send to school for the whole class when your child has a birthday.

Your child's favorite cake mix
18 flat-bottomed ice cream cones
Frosting
Cake decorations

Make your child's favorite cake mix according to the package directions. Place 18 cones in muffin tins and fill them half full with cake mix. Cook the Cone Cakes at 350° F for about 15 minutes, until the cake mix begins to pull away from the sides of the cones. Frost and decorate the cones. The cake will probably rise to a point just below the lip of the cone, so you'll be able to keep the frosting below the lip of the cone, which makes these cone cakes easier than conventional cupcakes to pack in a lunch box.

Yield: 18 cone cakes

Berry Puree

• • •

Here's a good dessert to consider if you're strongly opposed to sugary desserts. The berries look beautiful and will hold up well in your child's lunch box. You can use as much or as little sugar as you see fit. You can use just one kind of berry or a mixture.

1/2 cup fresh or frozen berries—
strawberries, blueberries,
raspberries, and so on

Sugar to taste
1 ice cube

Put all the ingredients in a blender and give 'em a whirl. Whip up this dessert just before your child leaves for school and put it immediately in a prechilled thermos. When it's first made, Berry Puree will be icy, like a sherbet. By the time your child sits down to eat, some of the ice will have melted, but the puree will still be nice and cold. Alternatively, you can whip up the berries and sugar (omit the ice cube) and freeze them overnight in a thermos. Then just pack the frozen dessert in your child's lunch box.

Passover Cookies

These tasty cookies have no leavening so they're a good choice for the Jewish holidays. If you can't find ground almonds at the market, buy slivered almonds and grind them in the blender.

3/4 cup margarine
1/2 cup sugar
1 1/4 cups all-purpose flour
1/4 cup ground almonds
1/2 teaspoon ground cinnamon

Peanut Butter Cookies

These cookies are yummy and the peanut butter fills them with protein.

1/2 cup margarine
1 cup sugar
1 egg
1 teaspoon vanilla
1 cup peanut butter
1 1/2 cups all-purpose flour
1/2 teaspoon baking soda
1/2 teaspoon salt

In a large bowl, mash the margarine with the back of a fork. Beat in the sugar, egg, and vanilla. Add the peanut butter and blend to a smooth paste. In a medium-size bowl, combine the flour, baking soda, and salt. Add the flour mixture a little at a time to the peanut butter mixture, until you have a smooth but not crumbly dough. Roll the dough into balls, about 1 inch in diameter. Space the balls on a greased cookie sheet and flatten them with the back of a fork, in a cross-hatch pattern. Bake at 375° F for about 10 minutes.

Yield: About 4 dozen cookies

St. Patrick's Day Popcorn Balls

• • •

Your child's friends will be "green with envy" when he pulls out this treat on St. Patrick's Day! On other days of the year, you may want to use different colors.

1/2 cup water
1 cup sugar
1/4 teaspoon cream of tartar
1 tablespoon margarine
1/2 teaspoon baking soda
A few drops green food coloring
4 to 6 cups popped corn

Heat water to boiling in a medium-size saucepan. Stir in the sugar and the cream of tartar. Cover the pan and let the mixture simmer over medium heat about 5 minutes. Remove the lid and continue cooking until the mixture turns pale yellow. Stir in the margarine and baking soda. Add a few drops of food coloring. Pour the green mixture over the popcorn and toss. When the popcorn is cool enough to handle (but still warm), shape it into balls 3 to 4 inches in diameter. Wrap the balls in waxed paper and refrigerate them until they harden.

Yield: 12 to 18 popcorn balls

In a medium-size bowl, mash the margarine with the back of a fork. Beat in the sugar and slowly add the flour, almonds, and cinnamon. Roll the dough into golf ball–size pieces and place them on a greased cookie sheet. Use your thumb to make a shallow indentation on each cookie. Bake at 350° F for about 15 minutes.

***Yield:* About 3 dozen cookies**

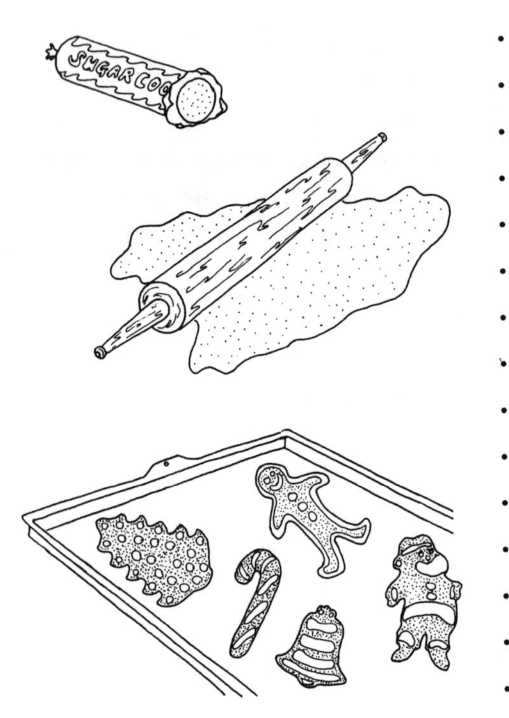

Christmas Cookies

• • •

December is the busiest time of the year for me. Even though I want to do everything just right and do all my baking from scratch (the way my mother always did), I just don't have the time. So this is how my daughter and I make our Christmas cookies. P.S. They taste great!

1 package (20 ounces) refrigerated sugar cookie dough

Several tubes of cake frosting

Cut off a chunk of cookie dough (about one-quarter of the tube) and roll the dough out on a floured surface to about $\frac{1}{4}$-inch thickness. Use cookie cutters to cut out holiday shapes. Bake the cookies on greased cookie sheets in a preheated 350° F oven for 5 to 10 minutes, until they start to brown around the edges. Let the cookies cool. Decorate them with the tubes of frosting.

Yield: About 2 dozen cookies

Chocolate-Covered Fruit

• • •

This dessert is a bit of a compromise. On the one hand, it's made with chocolate, but on the other hand, the main ingredient is wholesome fruit. It's an elegant treat for an adventurous eater.

1 tablespoon margarine
3/4 cup evaporated milk
6 ounces milk chocolate, broken into pieces
Chunks of fruit: pineapple, banana, apple, mandarin orange sections, strawberries, and so on

Over low heat, in a thick-bottomed pan, melt the margarine. Stir in the evaporated milk and the milk chocolate. Stir steadily until the chocolate melts and the mixture is rich, smooth, and creamy. Then turn off the heat. Skewer the chunks of fruit on toothpicks and dip them in the chocolate. Place the chocolate-covered fruit on waxed paper. When all the fruit is dipped, place it in the freezer to harden. When you're ready to send this dessert to school, put the fruit in a lidded plastic container and make sure your child's lunch box is cool, so the chocolate doesn't melt.

Granola Bars

These great-tasting bars will provide you with competition for the less healthful store-bought variety. Choose a granola that's low in fat and sugar.

3 eggs
1 teaspoon salt
1 teaspoon vanilla
1/2 cup brown sugar, packed (optional)
2 cups granola
3/4 cup peanuts (optional)

In a large bowl, beat the eggs well and then beat in the salt, vanilla, and optional brown sugar. Mix in the granola and peanuts, if desired. Spread this mixture into a greased 8×8-inch pan. Bake at 350° F for about 15 minutes. When the mixture has cooled, cut it into bars.

Yield: About 18 bars

Chocolate or Carob Chip Cookies

Coconut is the secret ingredient we put in chocolate chip cookies at our house to make them extra chewy. When we don't have time to make chocolate chip cookies from scratch, we buy a packaged mix and add chopped nuts and coconut.

1/2 cup margarine
1/2 cup brown sugar, packed
1/2 cup white sugar
1 egg
1 teaspoon vanilla
1 cup all-purpose flour
1/2 teaspoon baking powder
1/2 teaspoon salt
1/2 cup chocolate or carob chips
1/2 cup chopped walnuts, peanuts, pecans, or other nuts
1/2 cup shredded coconut

In a large bowl, mash the margarine with the back of a fork. Beat in the sugars, egg, and vanilla. In a medium-size bowl, combine the flour, baking powder, and salt. Add the flour mixture to the egg mixture and mix to blend. Stir in the chocolate or carob chips, chopped nuts, and shredded coconut. Drop by rounded teaspoonfuls onto greased cookie sheets. Bake at 375° F for about 10 minutes.

Yield: About 4 dozen

Discovering Carob

Kids love chocolate and most kids can handle it in moderation, but it's really not a great food for children—or anyone else, for that matter. Chocolate is high in fat and contains the drug caffeine. Your local health food store may carry carob, which tastes something like chocolate but is very low in fat and contains no caffeine. Try substituting carob for chocolate powder in your favorite recipes, or experiment with using half chocolate and half carob. Or use carob chips in recipes that call for chocolate chips.

Carob Chip Bars

Your child won't know these yummy bars are made with carob chips unless you tell him.

3/4 cup margarine
1 cup sugar
1 teaspoon vanilla
1 egg
1/4 cup water
2 1/2 cups all-purpose flour
1 1/2 teaspoons baking powder
1/4 teaspoon salt
1 cup carob chips

In a large bowl, mash the margarine. Beat in the sugar, vanilla, egg, and water. In a medium-size bowl, mix the flour, baking powder, and salt. Add the flour mixture to the large bowl and mix. Fold in the carob chips. Spread the mixture in a greased 9×13-inch pan and bake at 350° F for about 25 minutes. When the mixture has cooled, cut it into bars.

Yield: About 3 dozen bars

Mini Fruit Pies

• • •

Here's a homemade alternative to those oh-so-popular packaged fruit pies—the ones with all the sugar and other additives. Look in the dairy section of your grocery store for a package of two pie crusts. Or buy a package of two frozen crusts and let them thaw.

1 cup fruit—chopped apples, pears, peaches, and so on, or fresh or frozen berries
Sugar to taste
¼ teaspoon ground cinnamon
2 premade 8-inch pie crusts
Milk

In a medium-size bowl, toss together the fruit, sugar, and cinnamon. (Omit the cinnamon if you're using berries.) Cut each pie crust in half down the middle. Spoon fruit onto half of each crust section. Dab milk around the edges of the crust. Fold the crust over the fruit. Use a fork to mash the edges of the crust together and to prick the top. Place on a lightly greased cookie sheet and bake at 375° F for about 15 minutes.

Yield: 4 pies

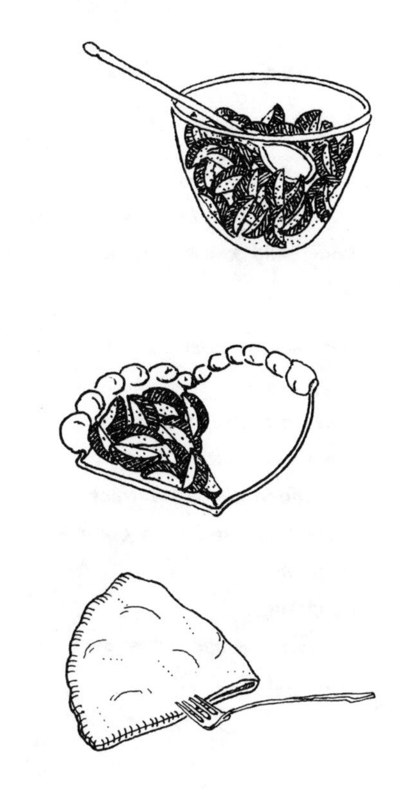

Valentine's Day Meringues

Here's a nice way to let your child know that he's your Valentine.

1 jar candied cherries
3 egg whites
1/4 teaspoon cream of tartar
1/8 teaspoon salt
1/2 teaspoon almond extract
A few drops red food color (optional)
3/4 cup sugar
2 cups sweetened shredded coconut

Peanut Butter and Banana Graham-Wiches

Here's a yummy treat that's fairly low in sugar. Pack it frozen in your child's lunch box—it'll still be cool by the time he sits down to eat.

1 ripe banana
1/3 cup peanut butter
Graham crackers

In a medium-size bowl, mash the banana with the back of a fork. Beat in the peanut butter. Break rectangular graham crackers into squares. Spread the squares with banana–peanut butter mixture and cover each square with another graham cracker. Wrap each "graham-wich" individually and pop them all in the freezer. Send them to school frozen.

Yield: About 6 graham-wiches

Ambrosia

• • •

The word *ambrosia* means "food of the gods," and many kids consider this fruity treat mighty heavenly. You can keep it sugar free or add marshmallows to make it even more appealing.

½ orange, sectioned and chopped
Sprig of grapes
½ banana, sliced
¼ cup shredded coconut
¼ cup miniature marshmallows (optional)
1 tablespoon orange juice

In a medium-size bowl, gently toss all the ingredients together. Pack the ambrosia in a lidded plastic container. Refrigerate for several hours until it is nice and cold. Be sure to send a spoon to school!

Yield: Two to three ½-cup servings

Cut the cherries in half. Then cut the cherry halves into heart shapes. Set them aside. In a large bowl, beat the egg whites, cream of tartar, and salt with an electric mixer until the egg whites are frothy. Beat in the almond extract and the red food color (to dye the cookies pink, if desired). Continue beating the egg whites and add the sugar, a little at a time, until the mixture is stiff. Gently fold in the coconut. Cover a cookie sheet with aluminum foil. Drop the cookie batter onto the foil by teaspoonfuls. Put a cherry heart in the center of each cookie. Bake at 300° F for about 20 minutes, until the edges start to brown.

***Yield:* About 3 dozen cookies**

Acknowledgments

Several friends helped me with this book. I especially want to thank Kathy Adler, Angela Henderman, Anne Lowenstein, Mary Jane Saffran, and Jackie Wertzer. I also want to thank my editors, Jane von Mehren, who suggested I write the book, and Irene Prokop. And I want to thank my daughter, Faith, for her help with the recipes.